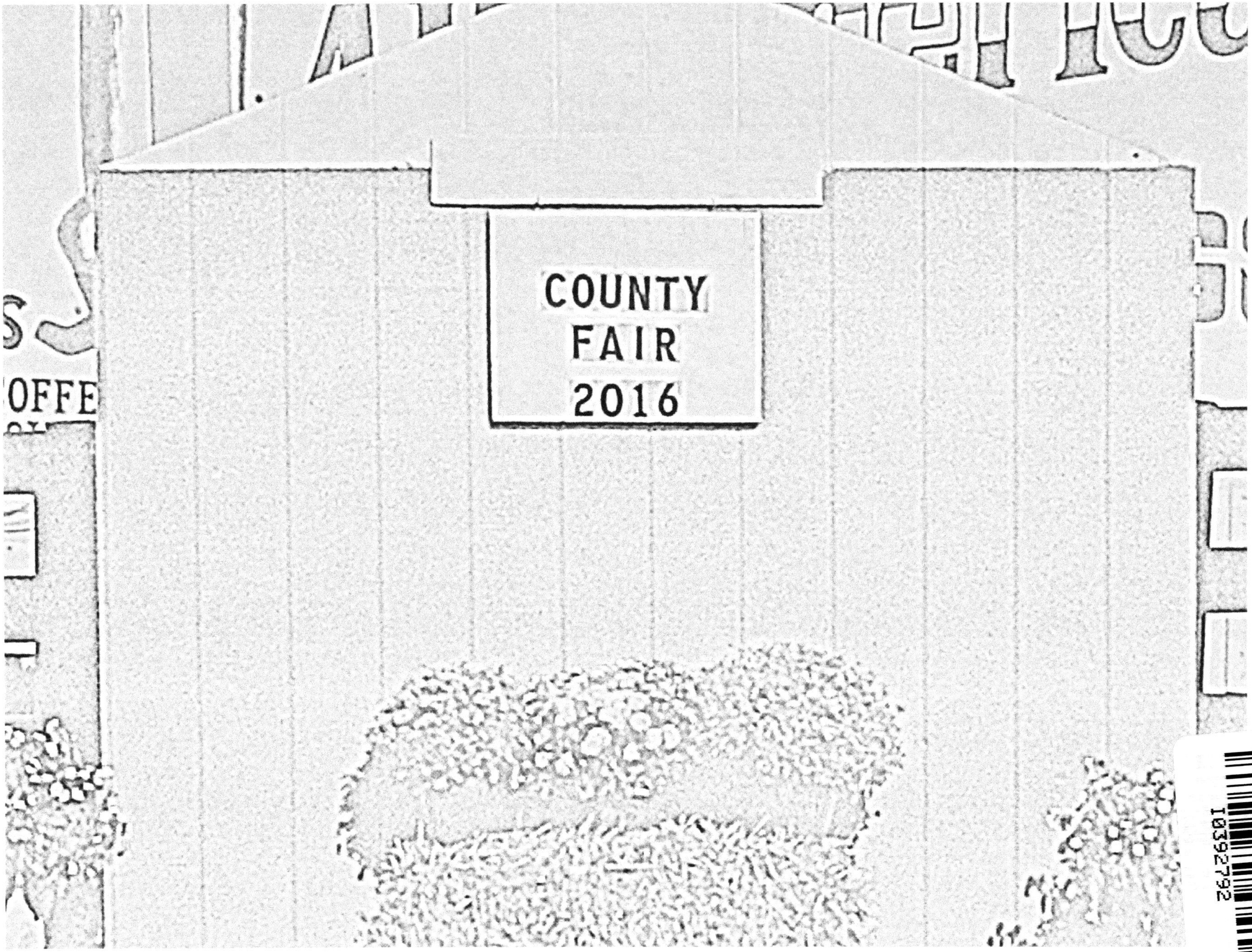
COUNTY
FAIR
2016

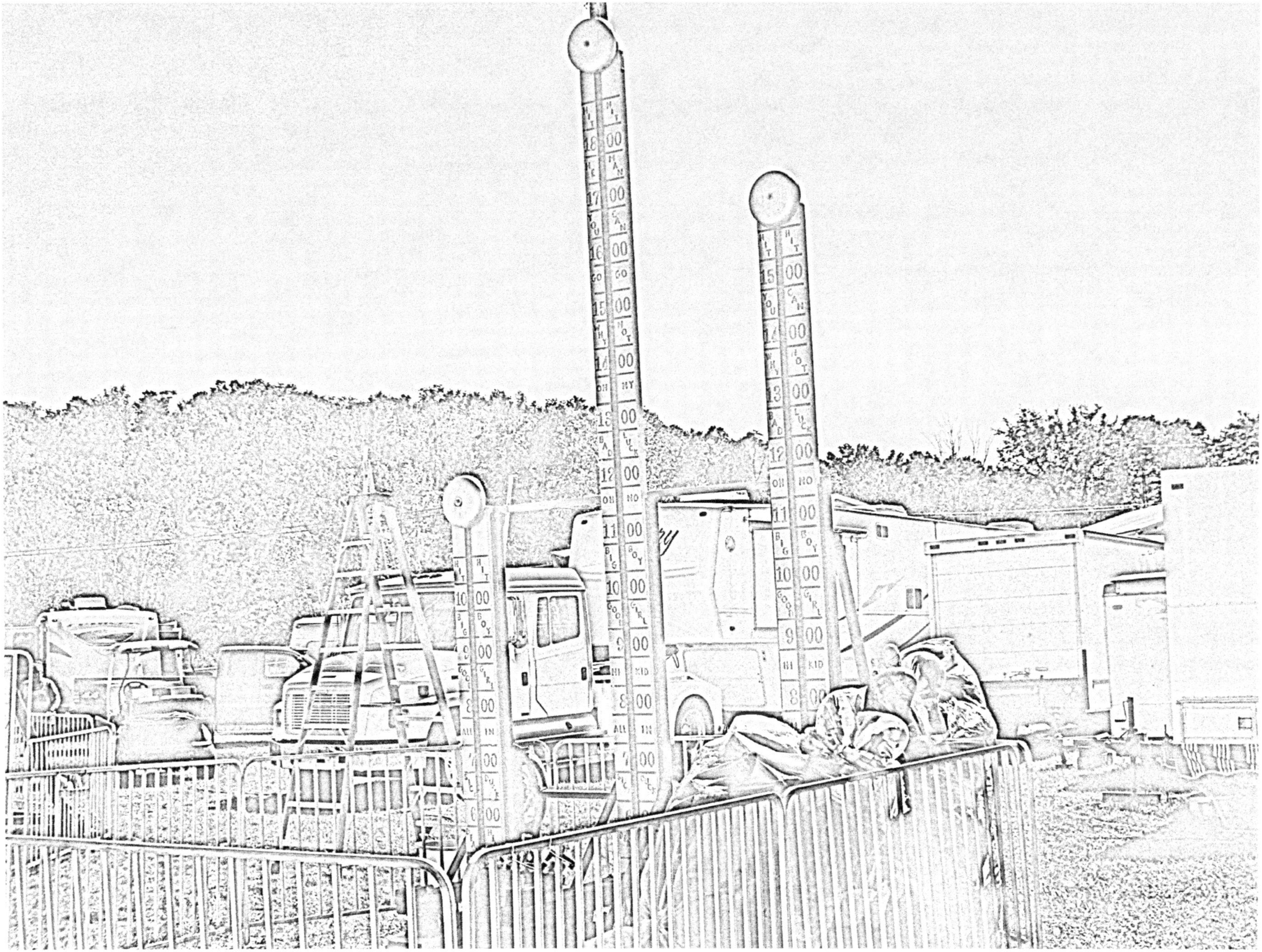
HIT
1800
1700
YOU CAN
1600
1500
1400
1300
BAD LUCK
1200
1100
BIG BOY
1000
GOOD GIRL
900
HI KID
800
ALL IN

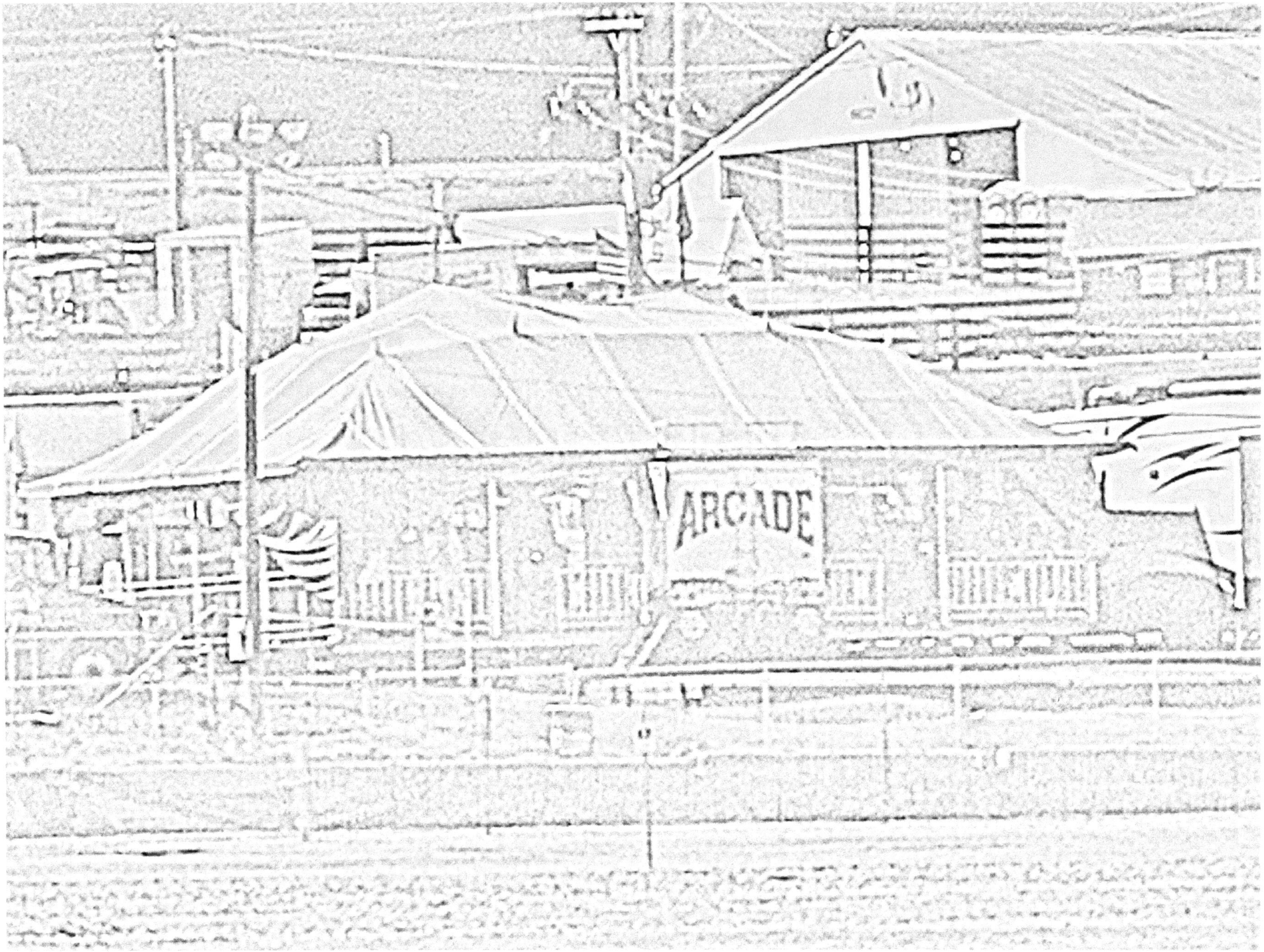
ARCADE

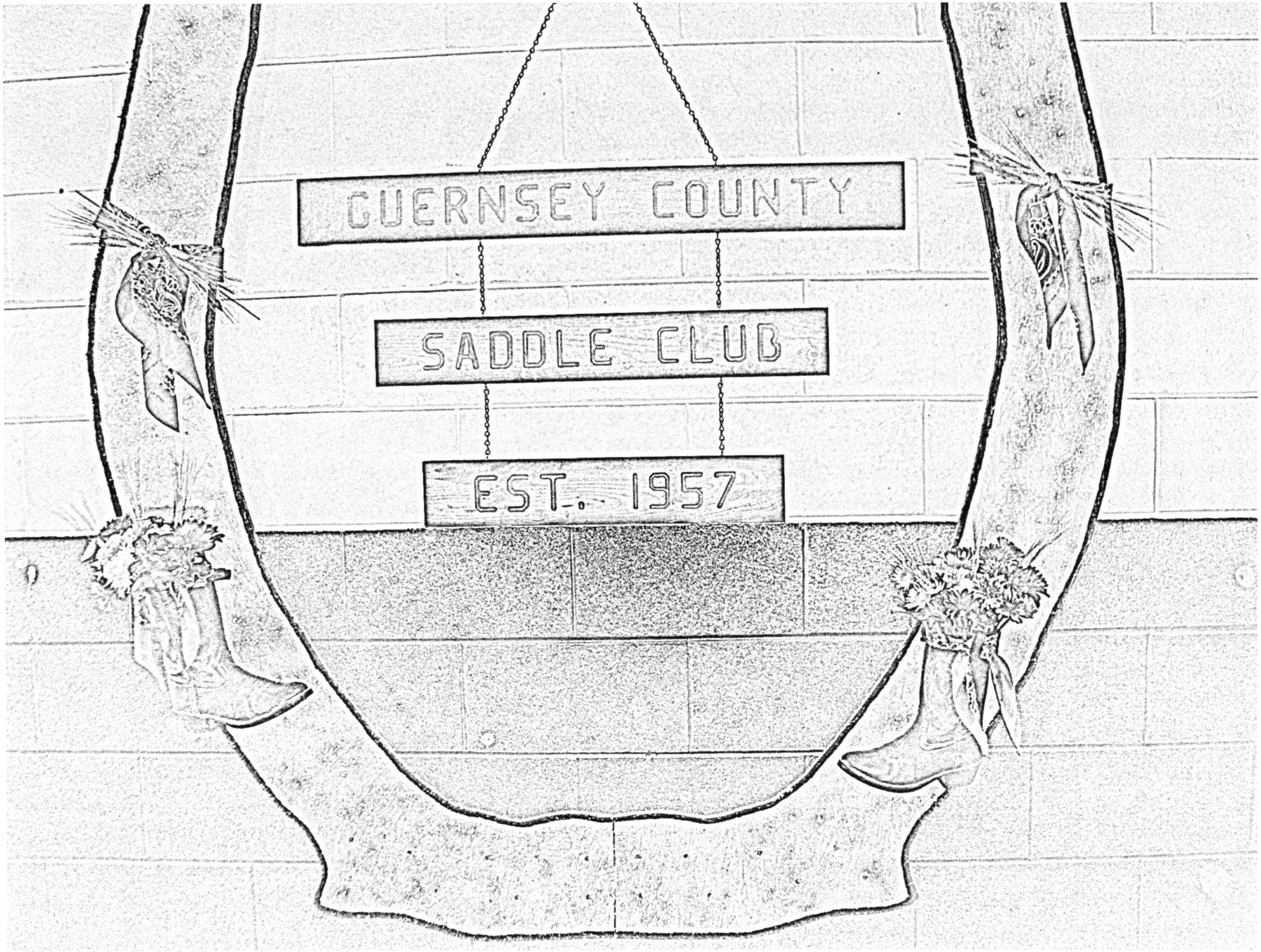
GUERNSEY COUNTY
SADDLE CLUB
EST. 1957

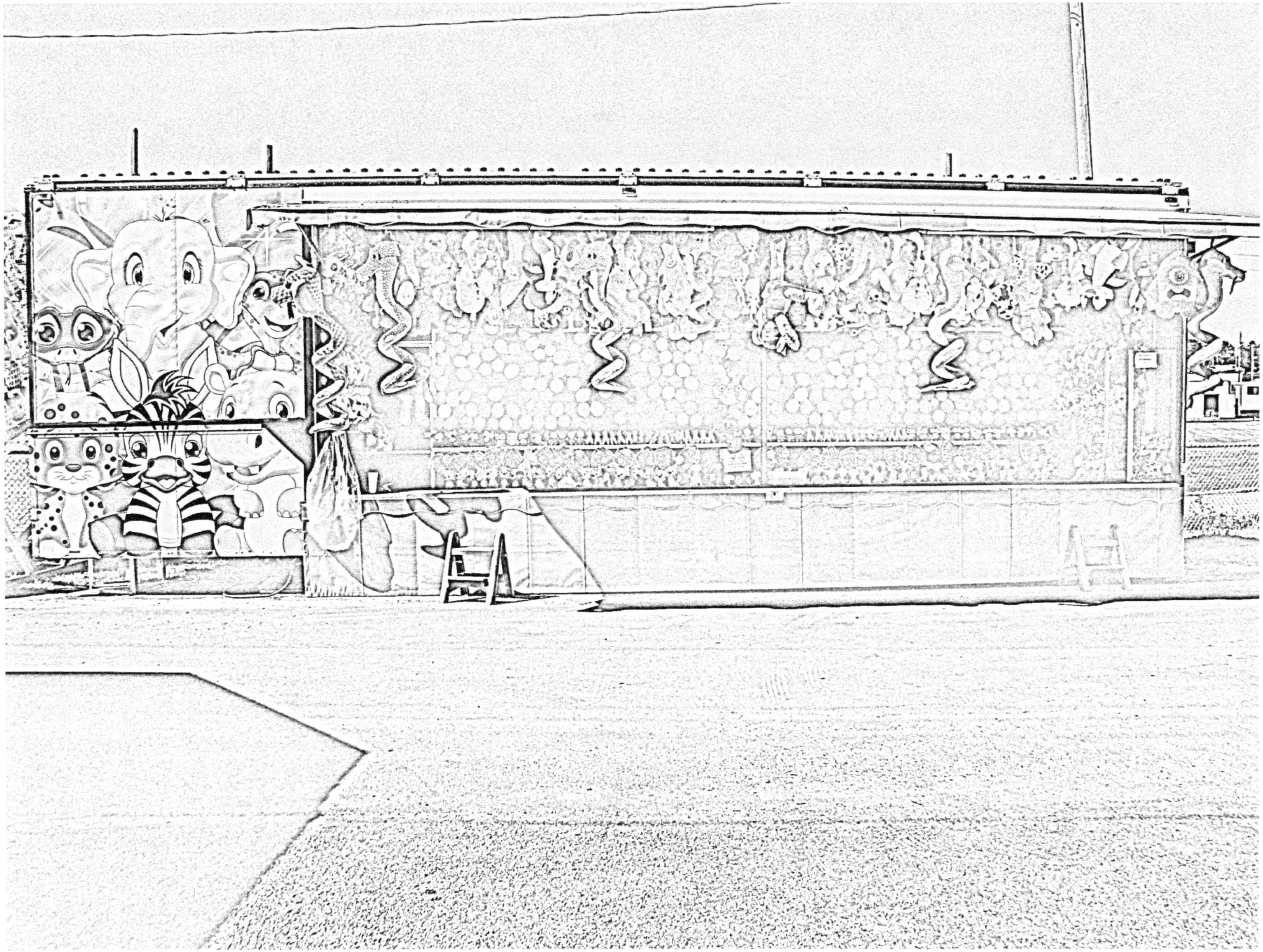

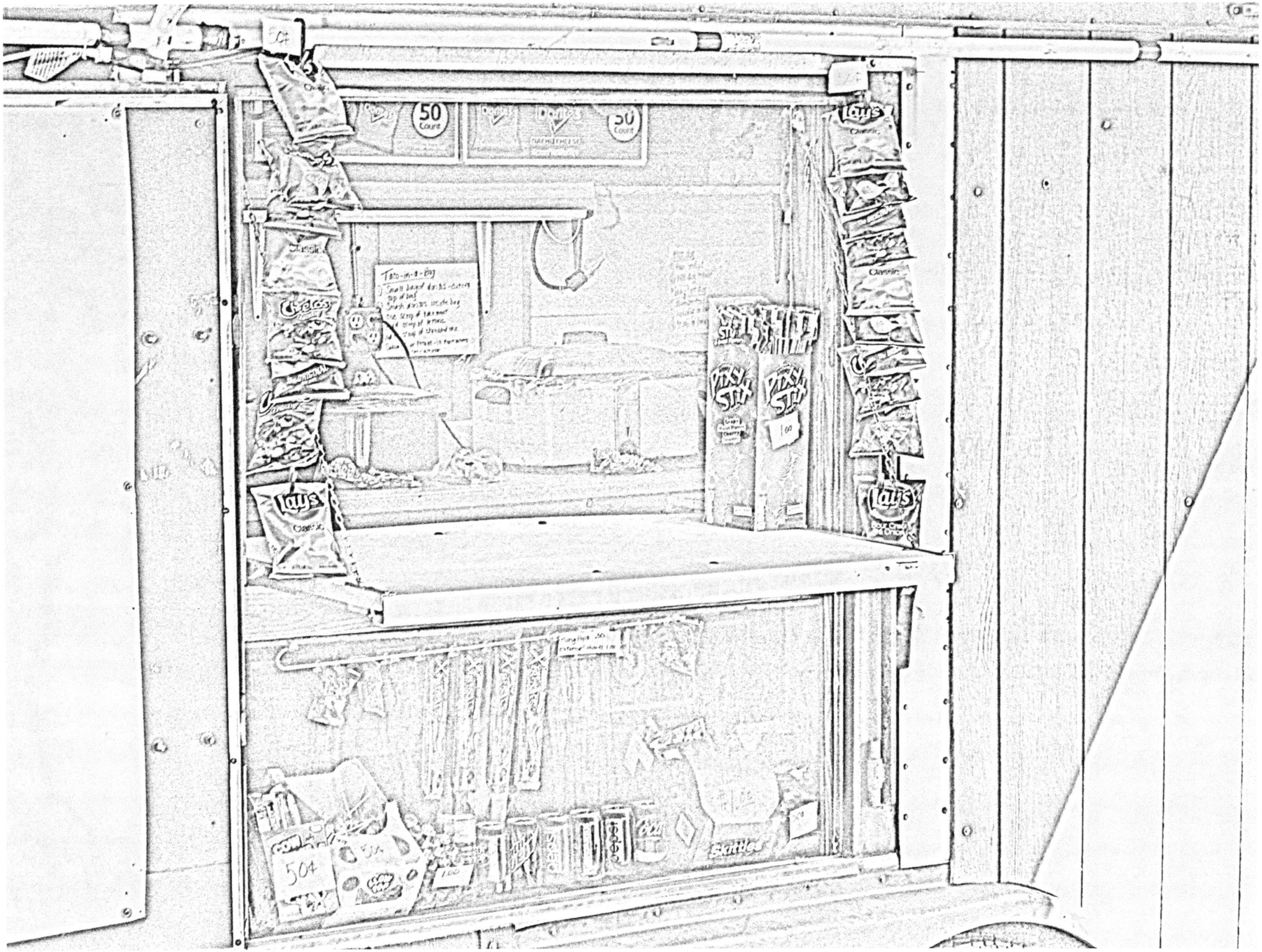

50¢
50 Count
50 Count
Lay's
Classic
Cheetos
Lay's
Classic
Pixy Stix
Pixy Stix
1.00
Skittles
50¢

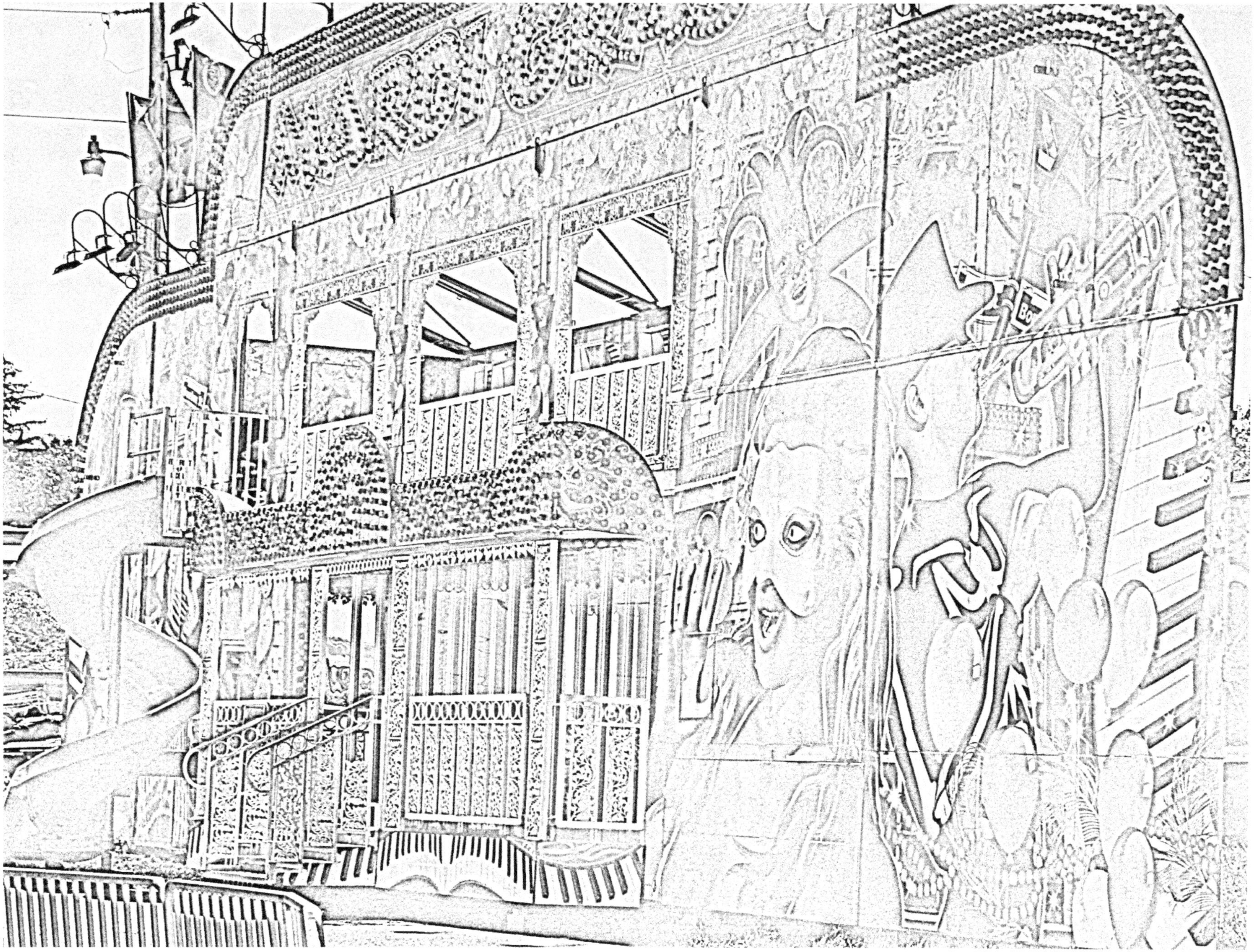

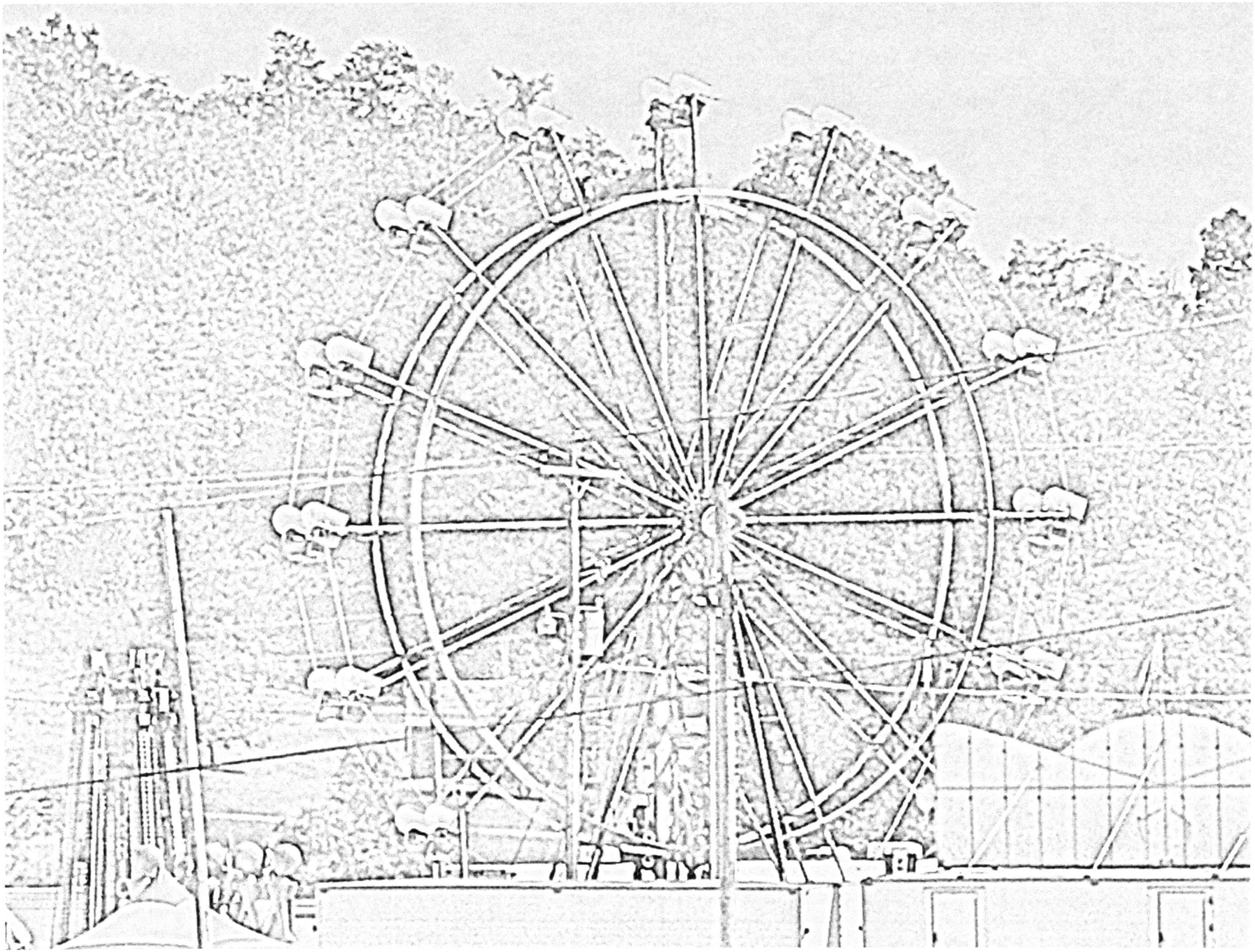

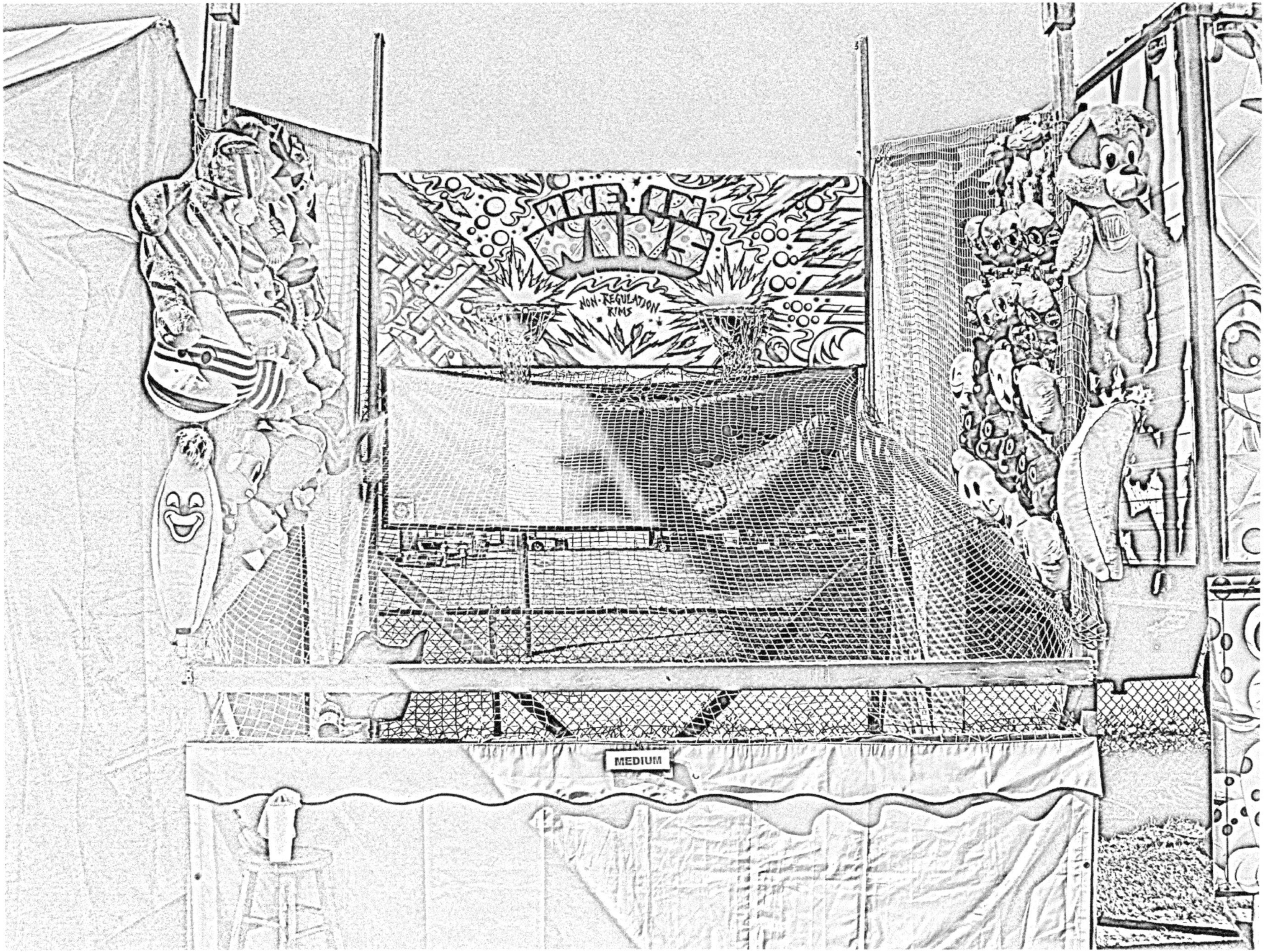
NON-REGULATION
RIMS
MEDIUM

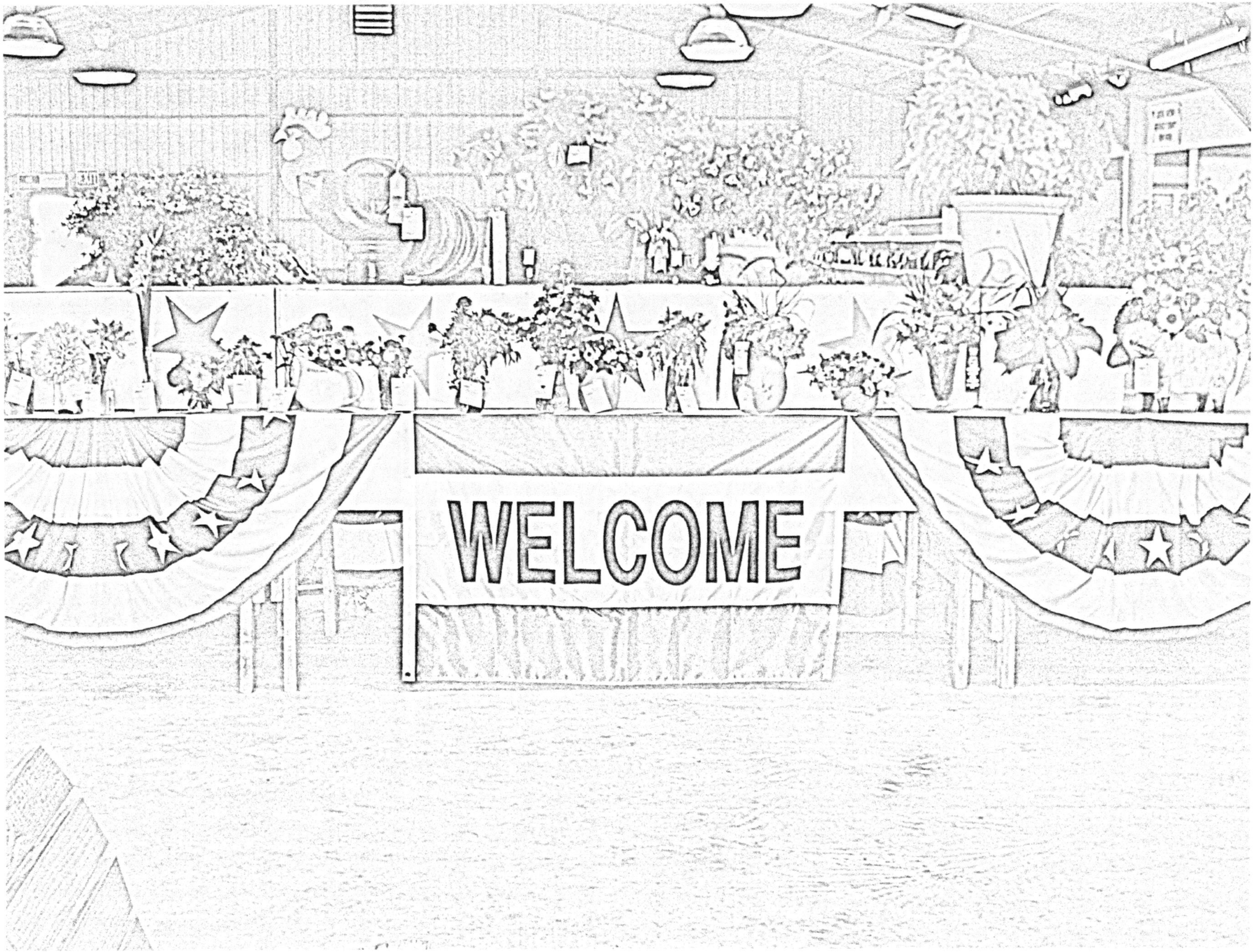
WELCOME

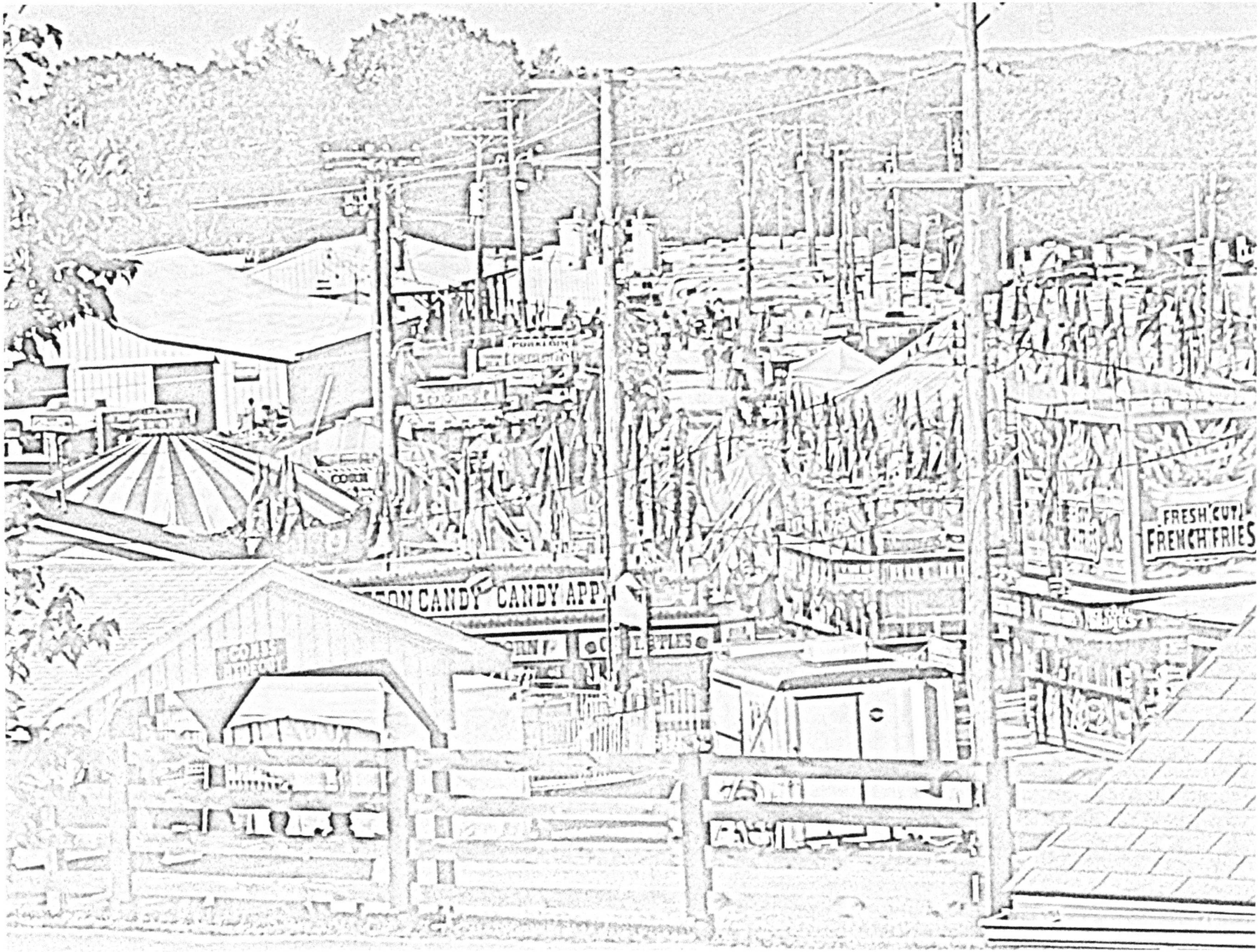
FRESH CUT
FRENCH FRIES
CANDY

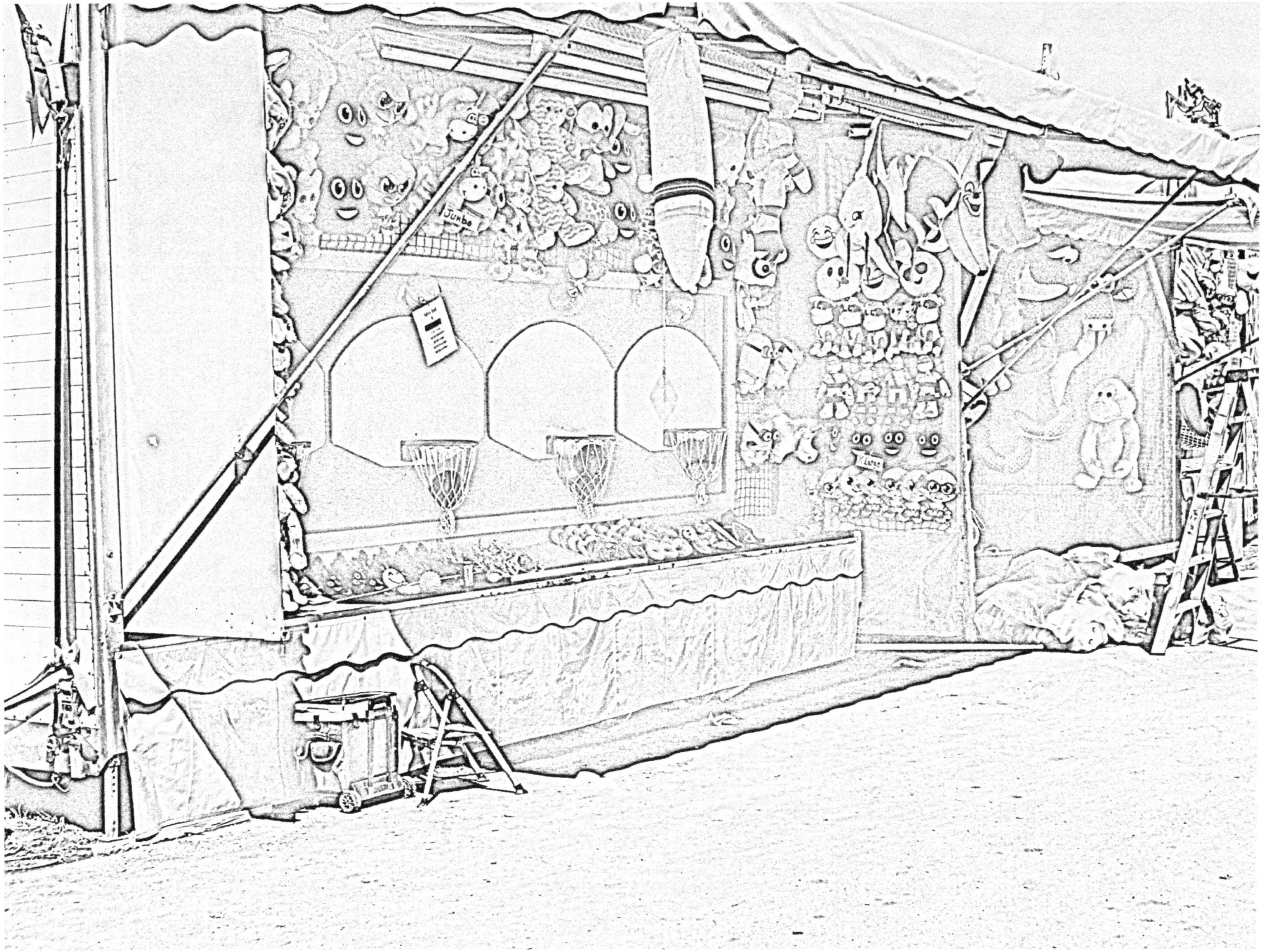
Jumbo

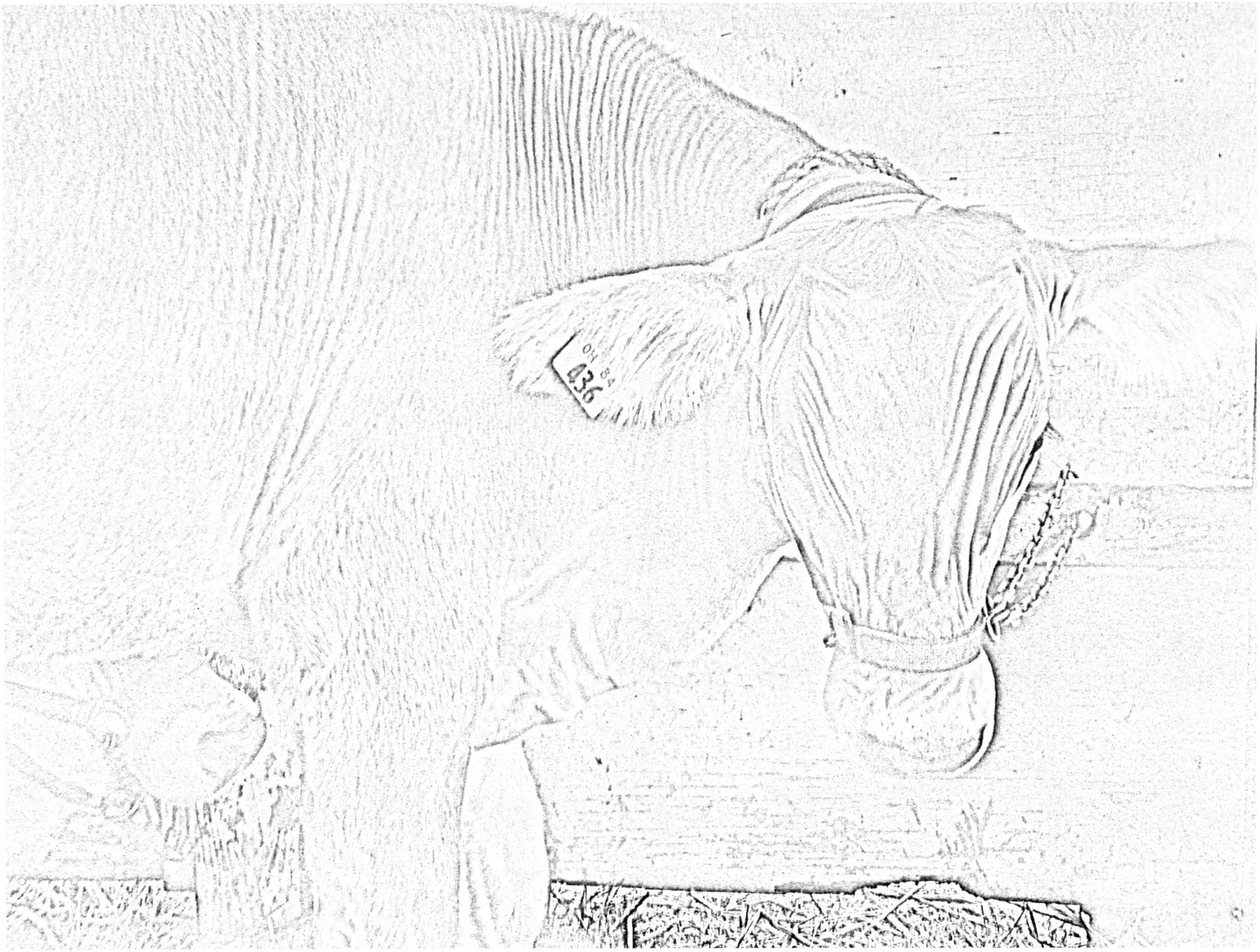
OH 84
436

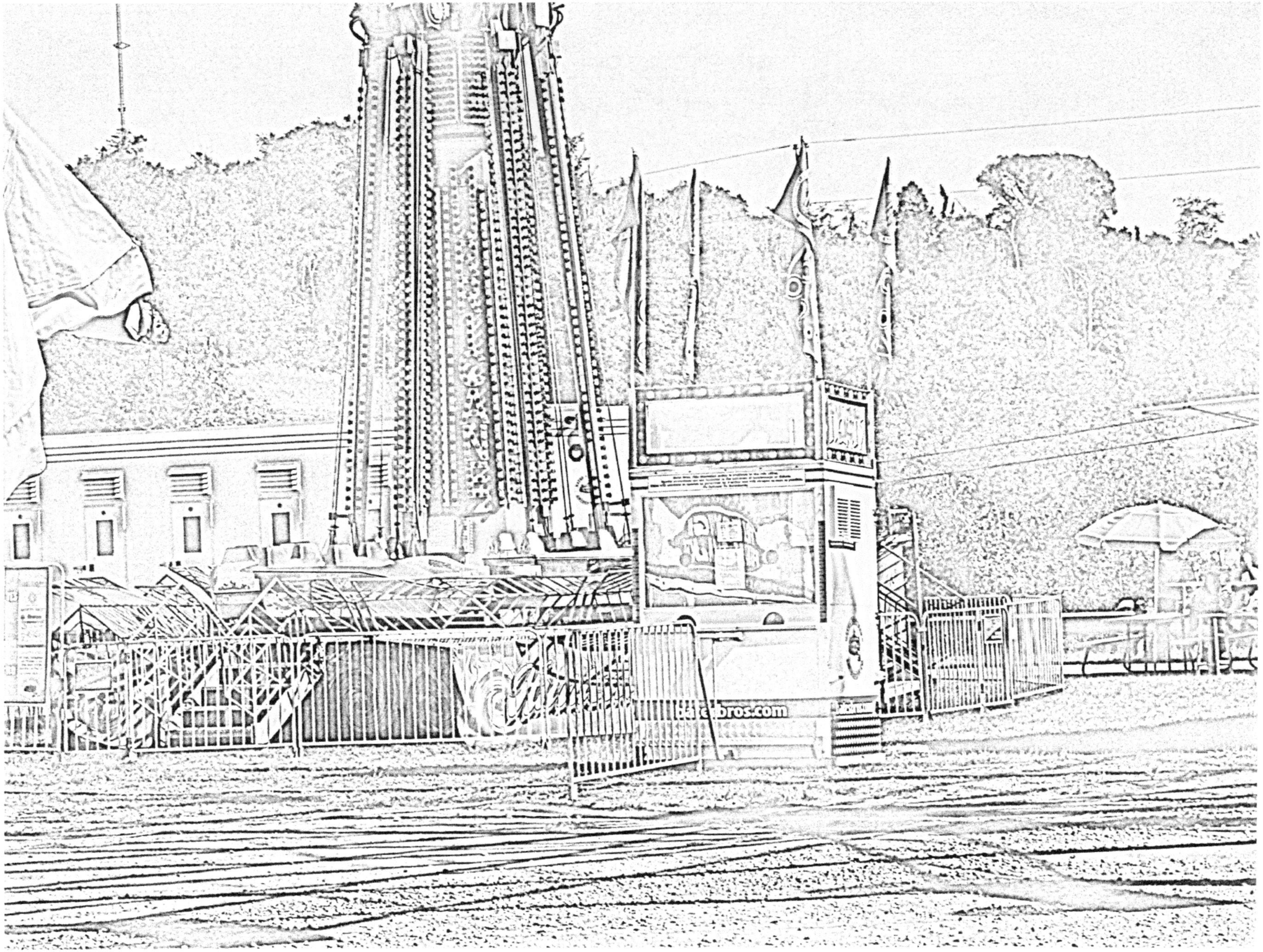
bros.com

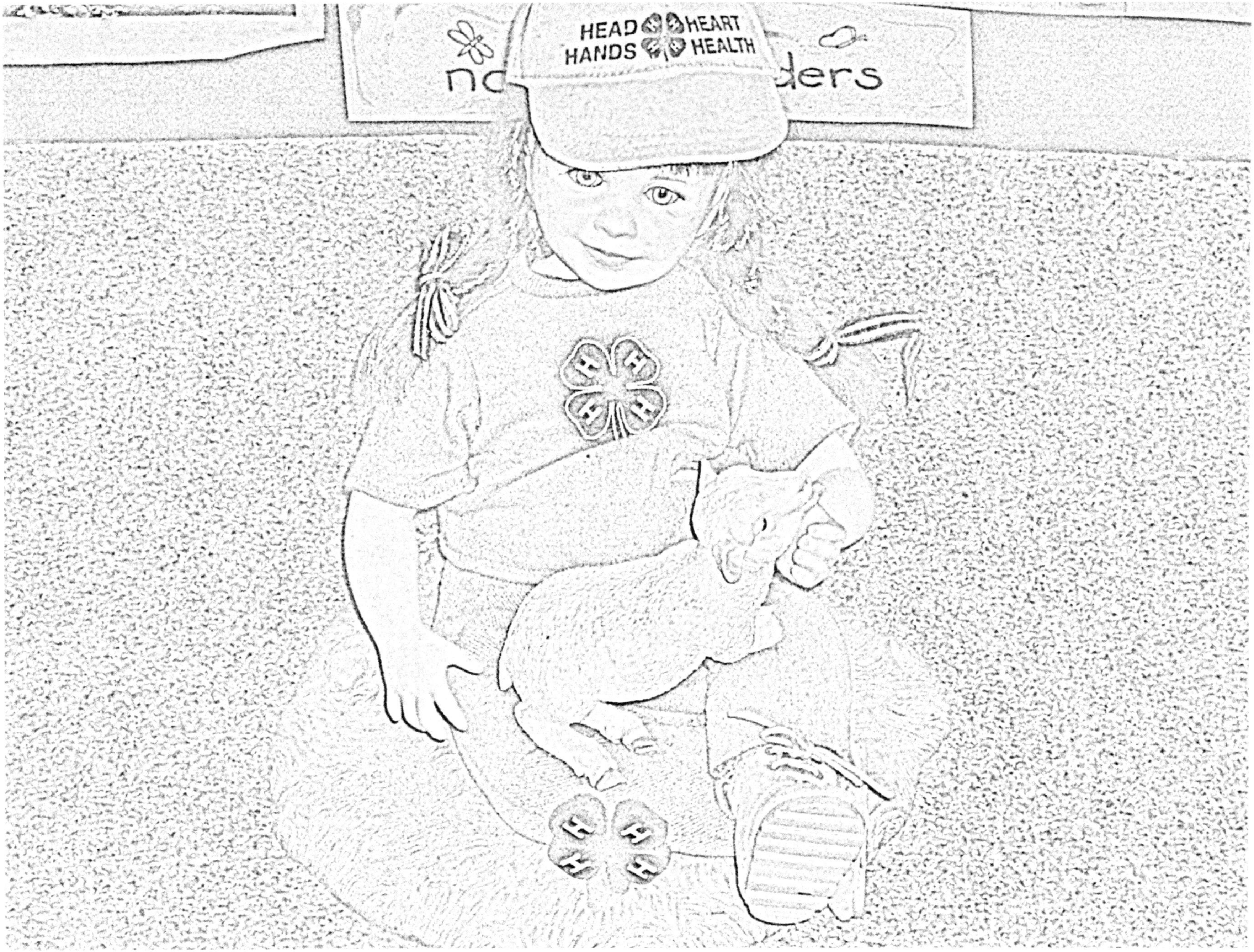
HEAD HEART
HANDS HEALTH

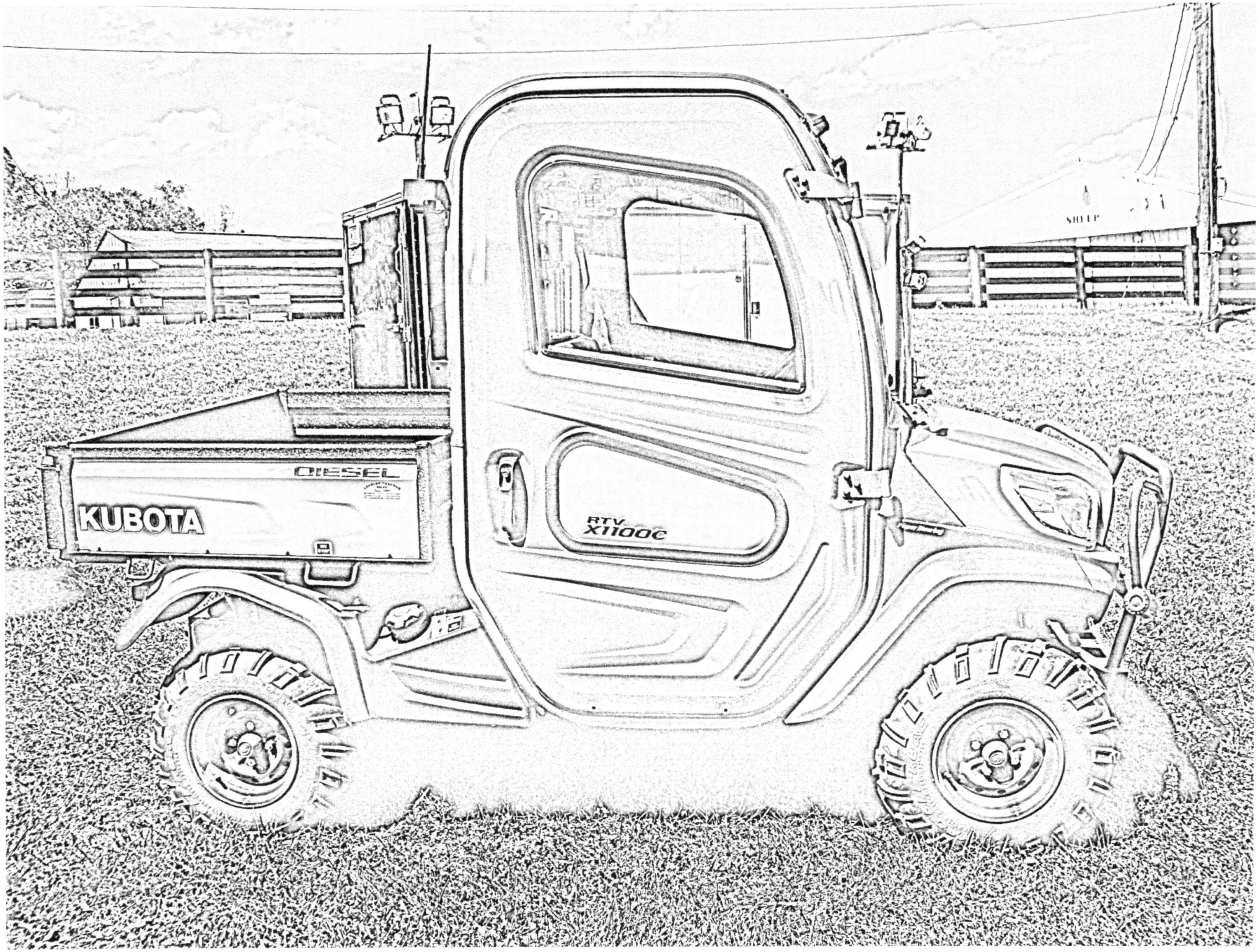
DIESEL
KUBOTA
RTV
X1100C

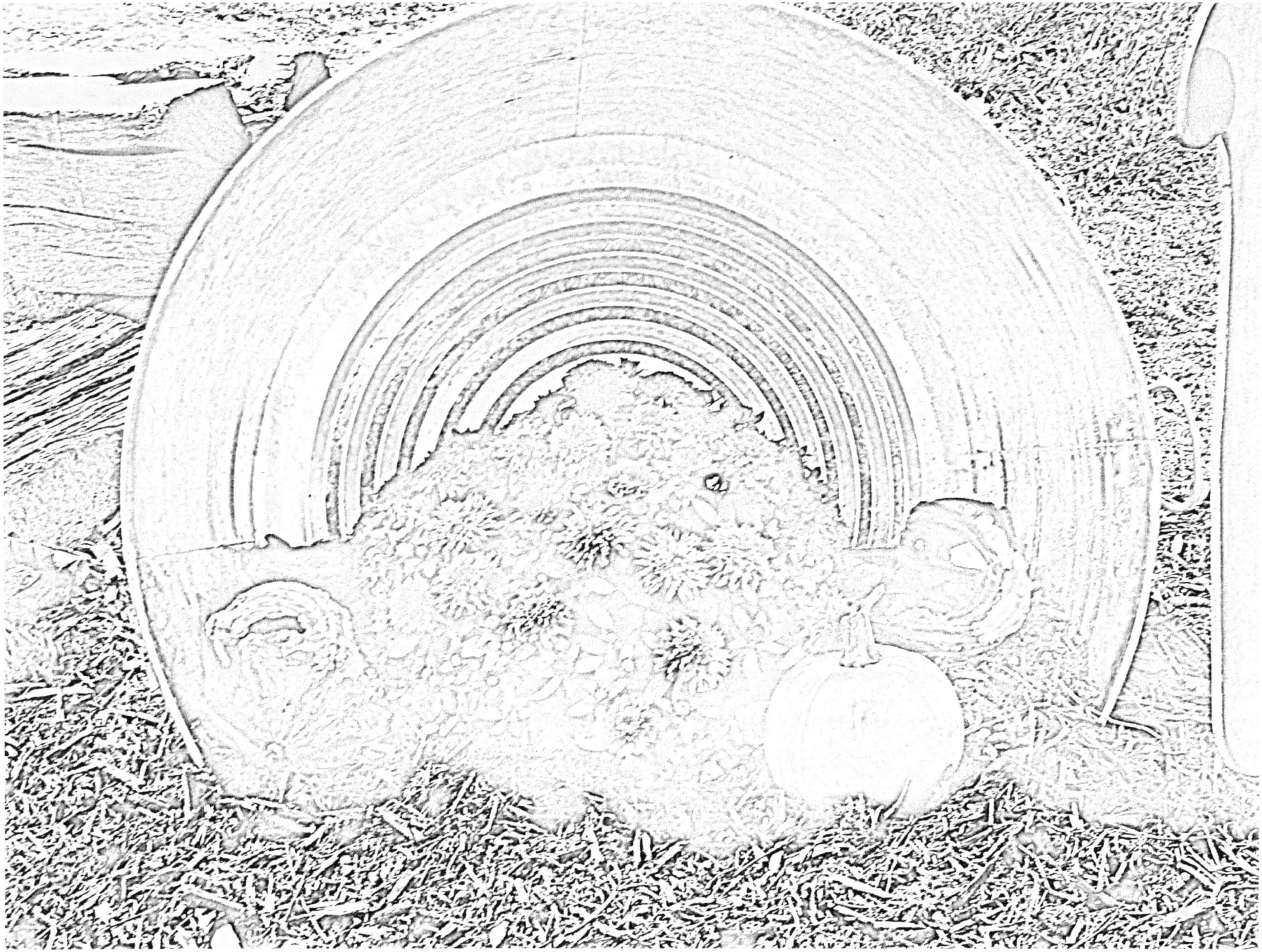

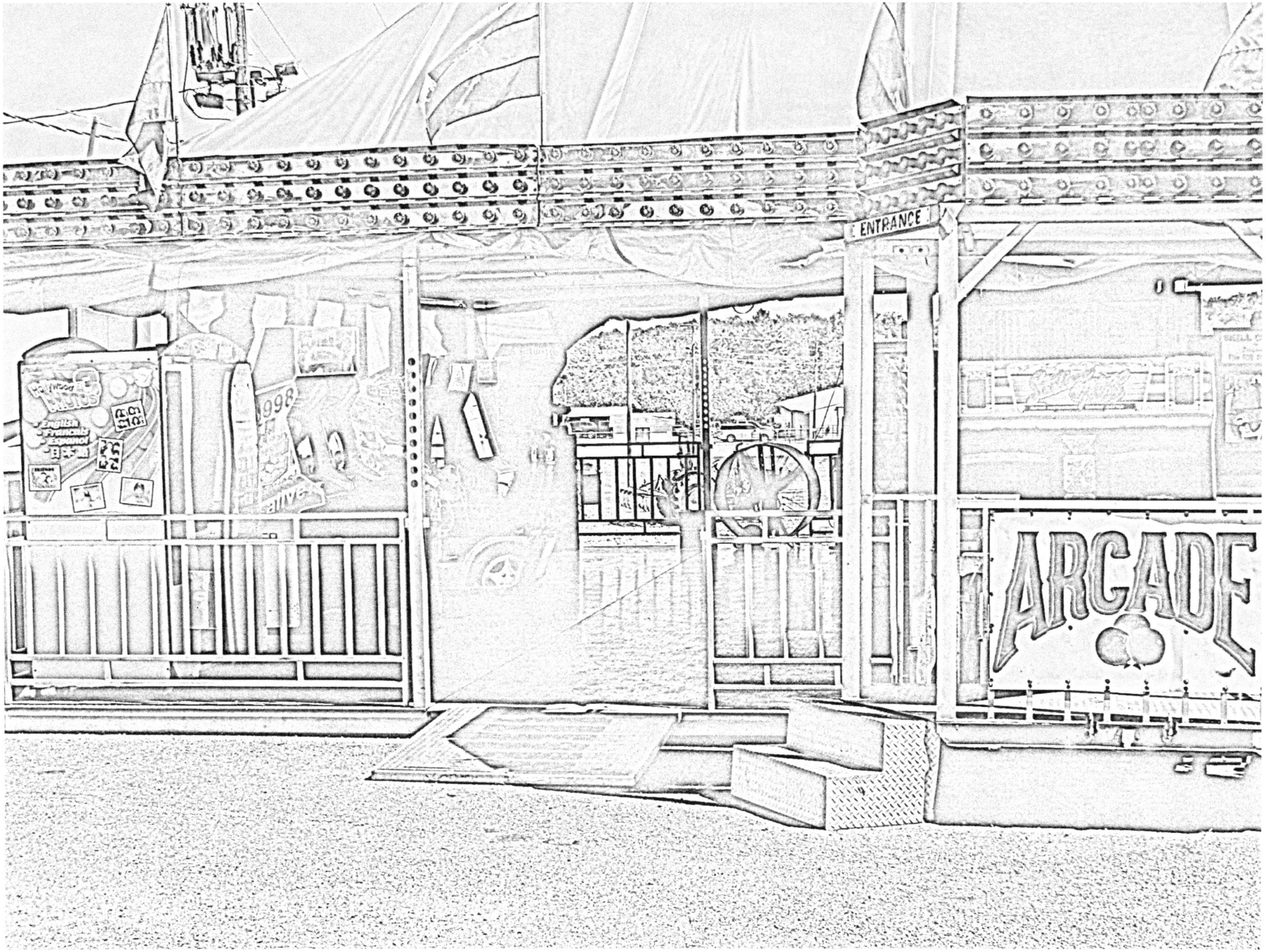
ENTRANCE
ARCADE

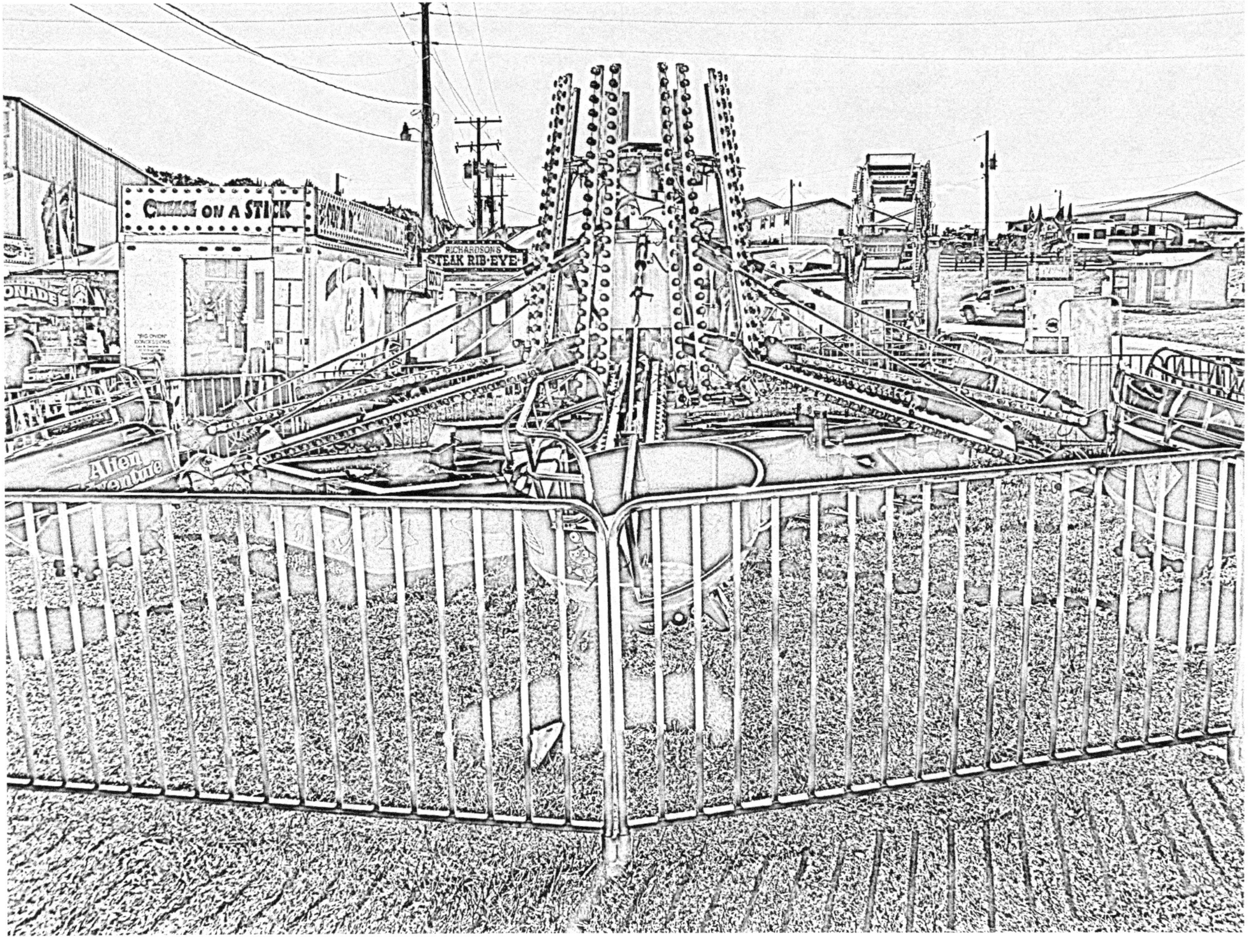
CHEESE ON A STICK
RICHARDSON'S
STEAK RIB-EYE
ONADE
Alien
Adventure

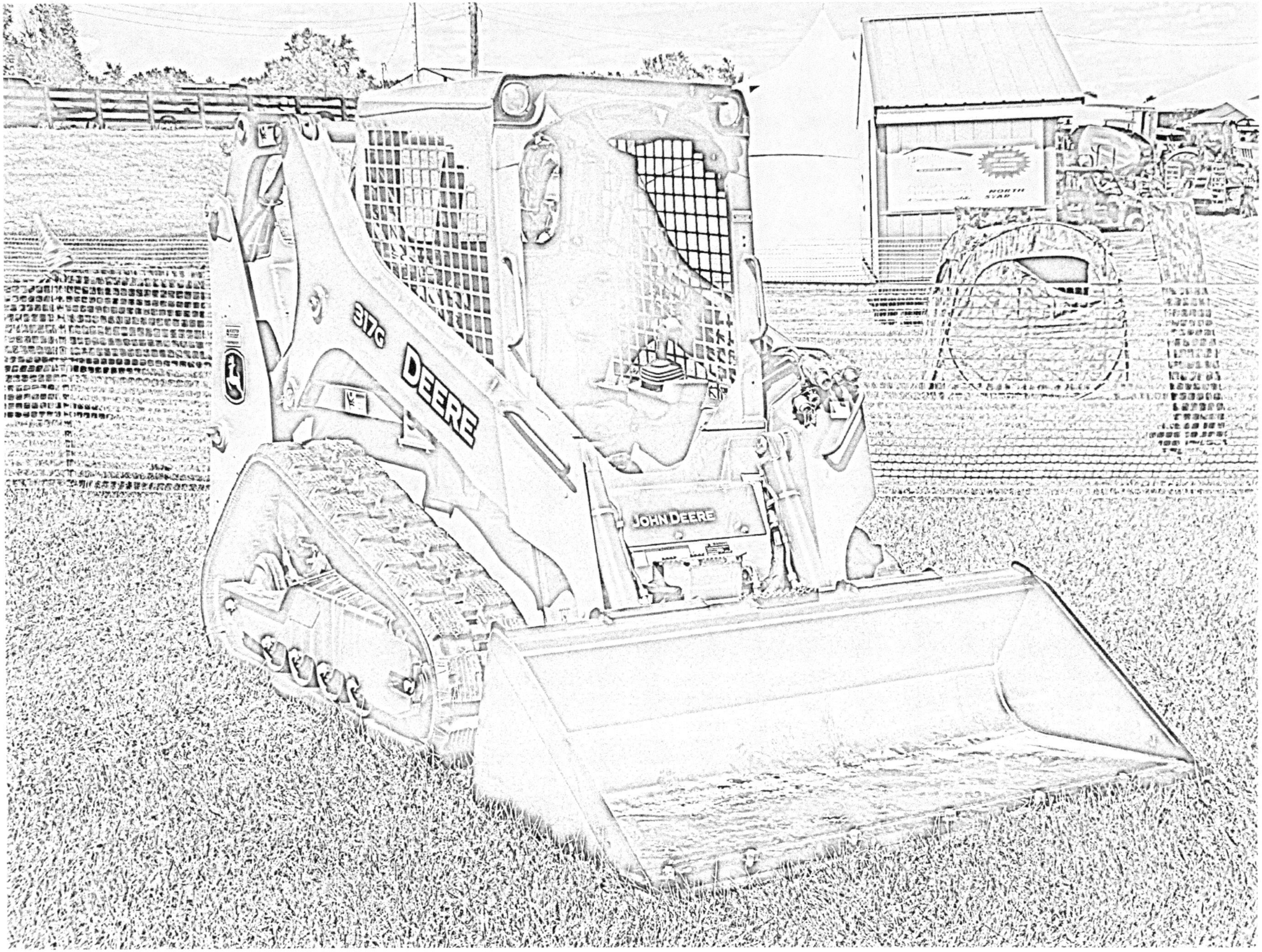
317G
DEERE
JOHN DEERE

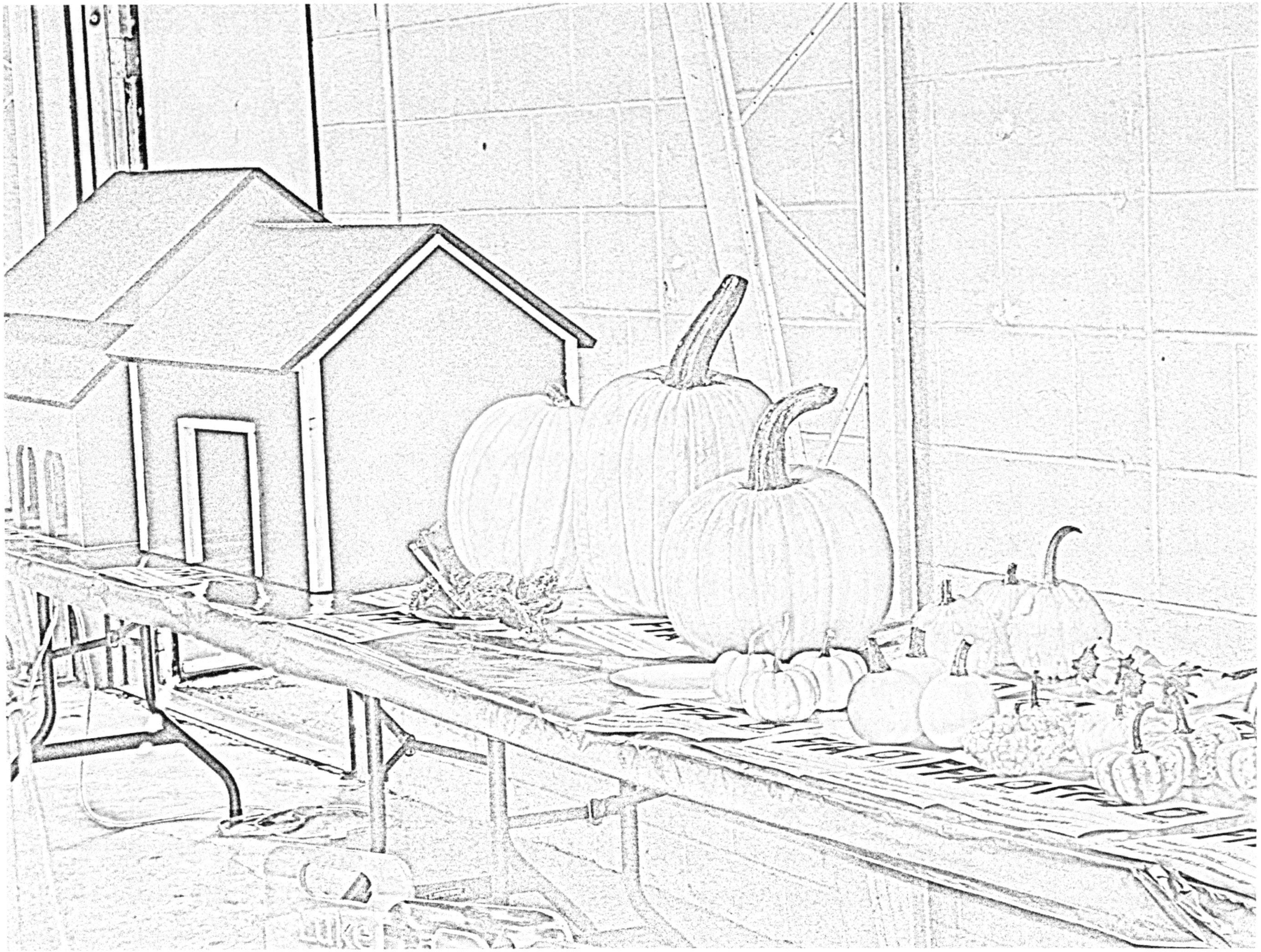

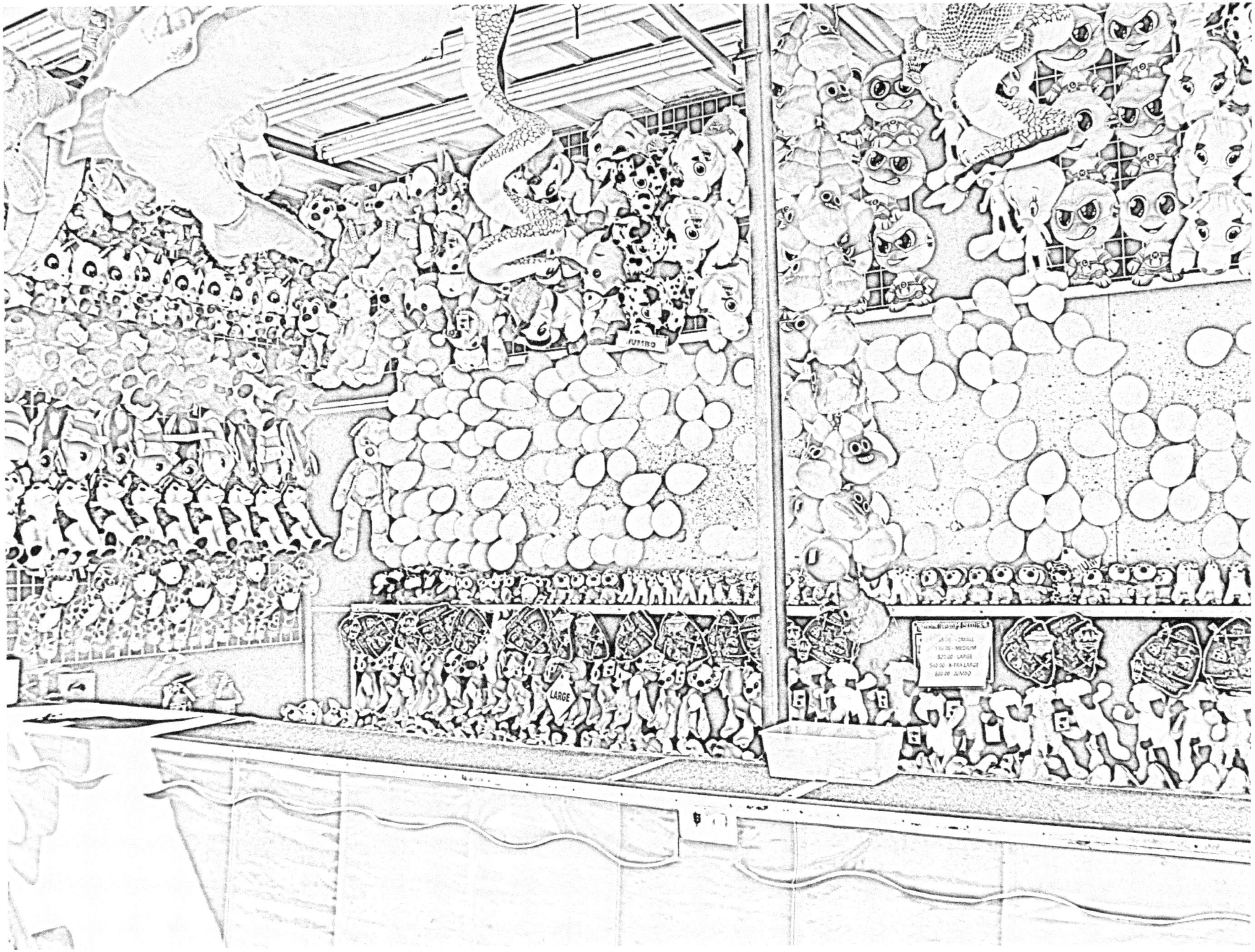
JUMBO
LARGE

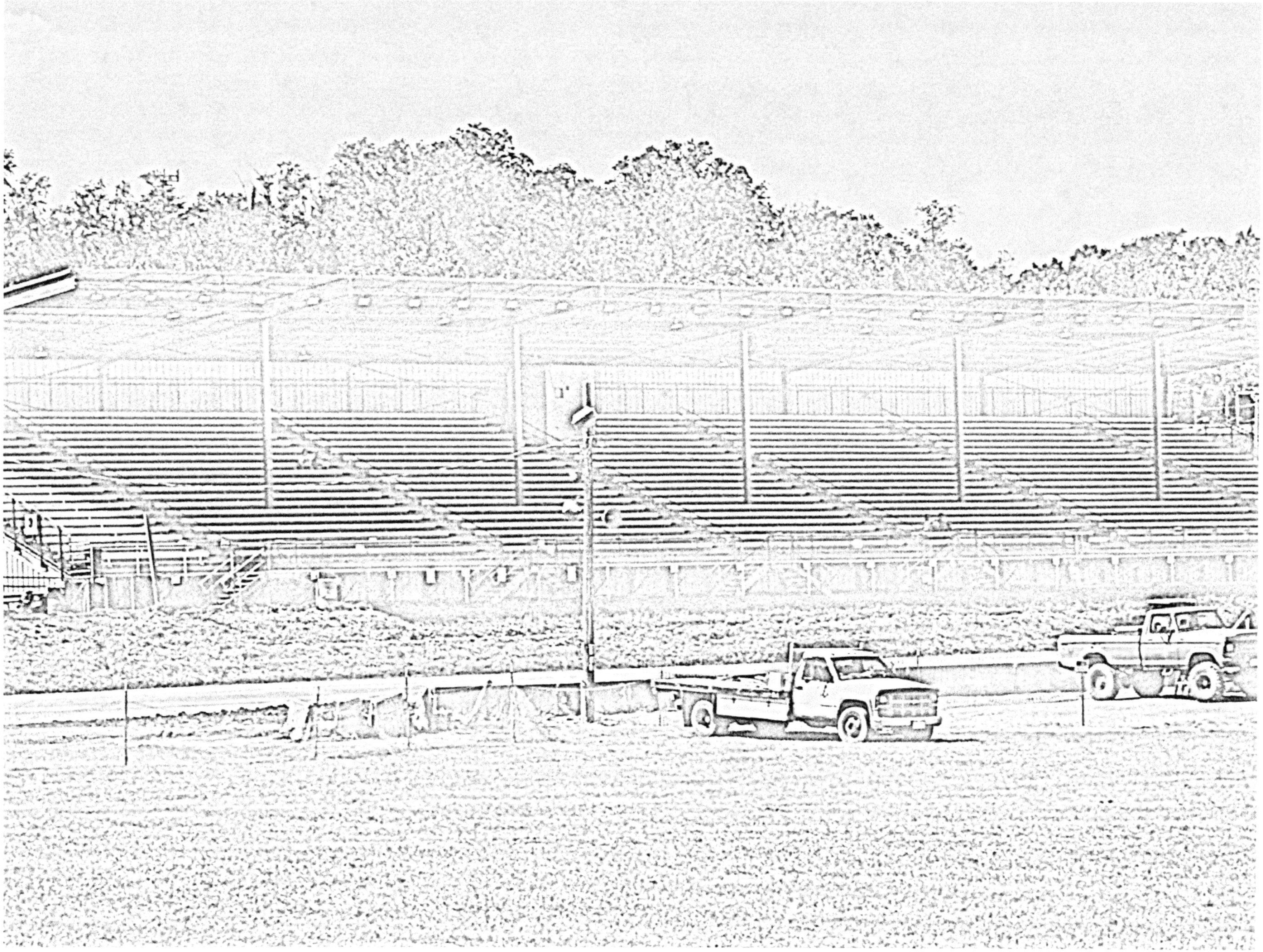

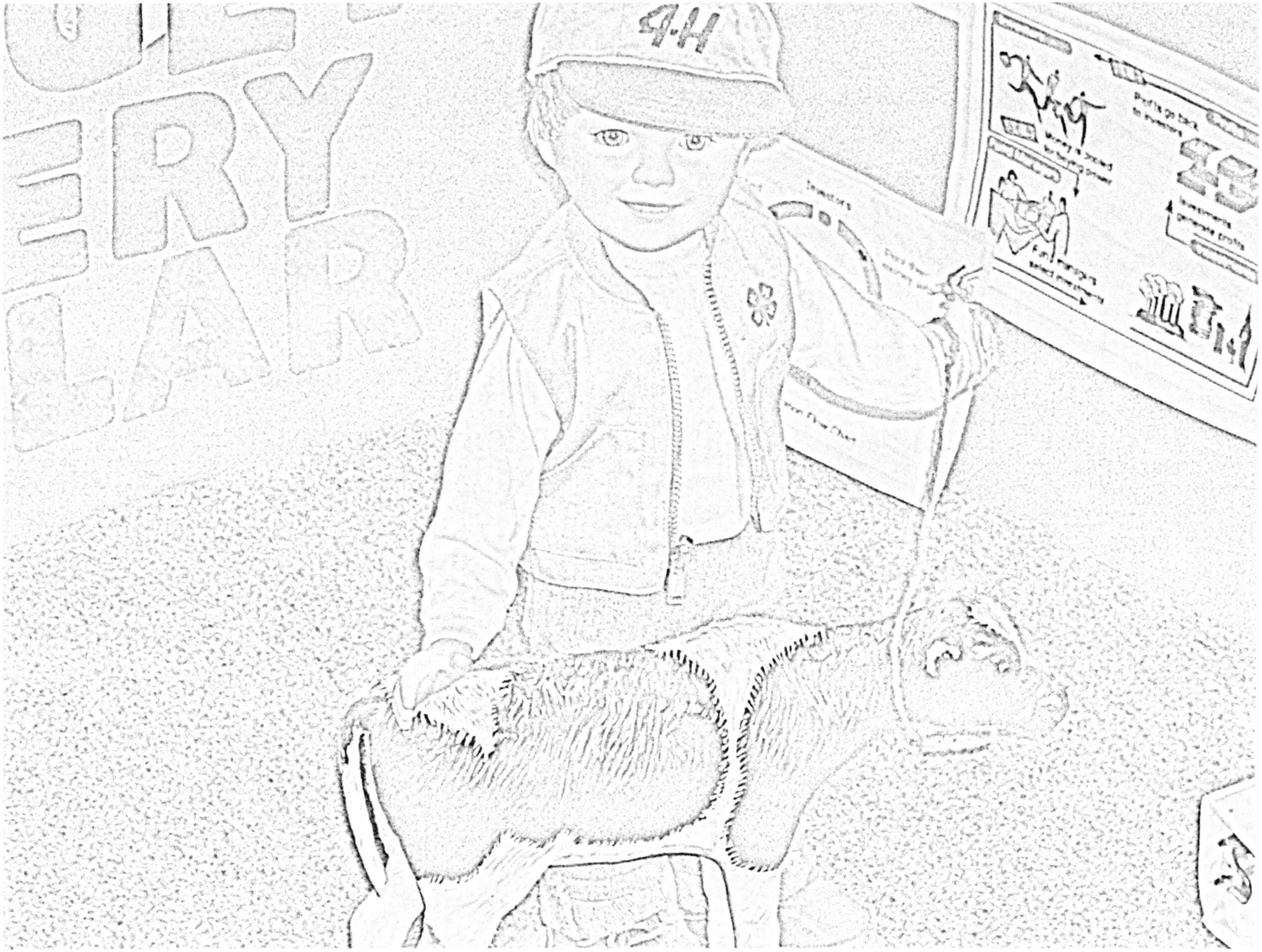
4-H

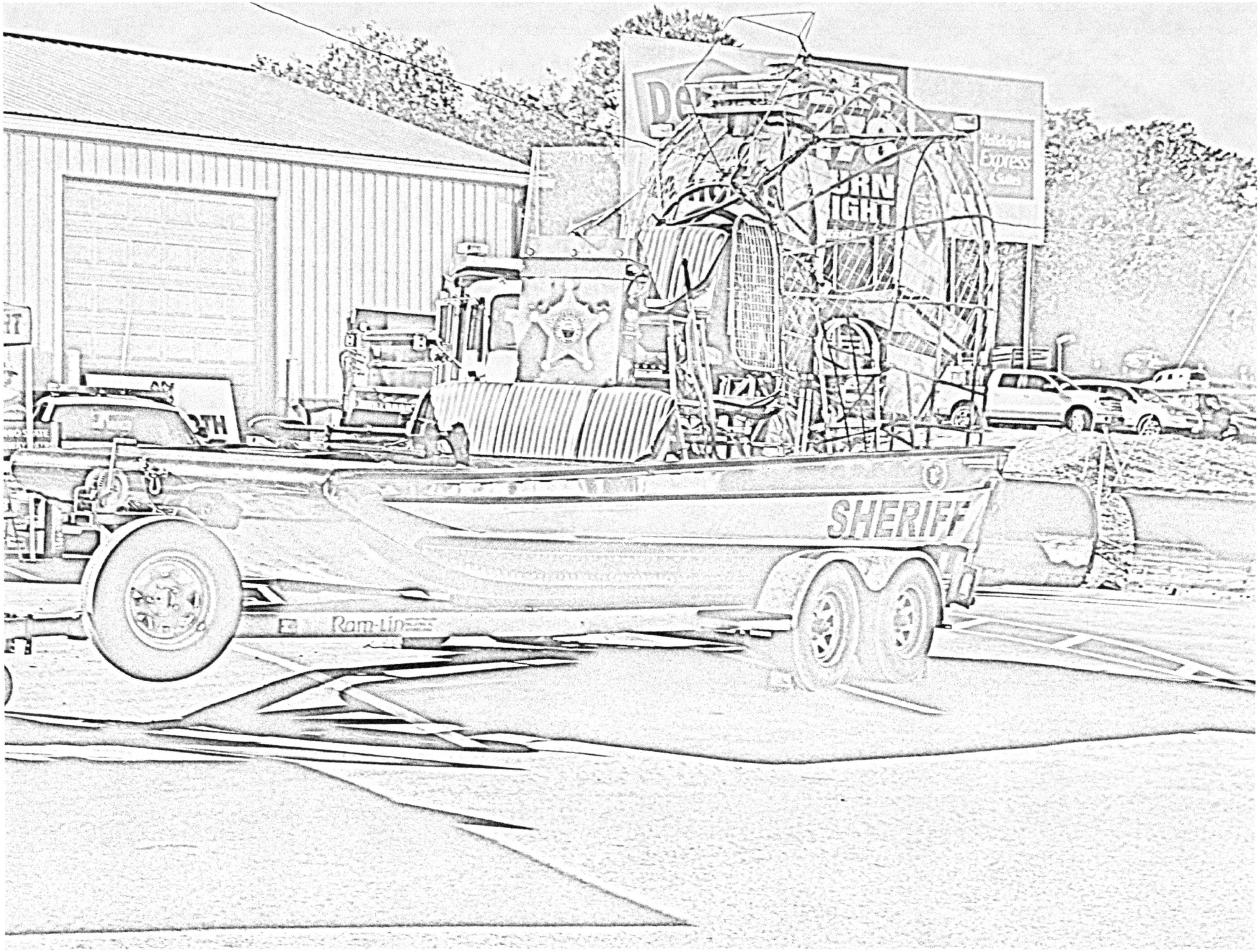
SHERIFF
Holiday Inn Express

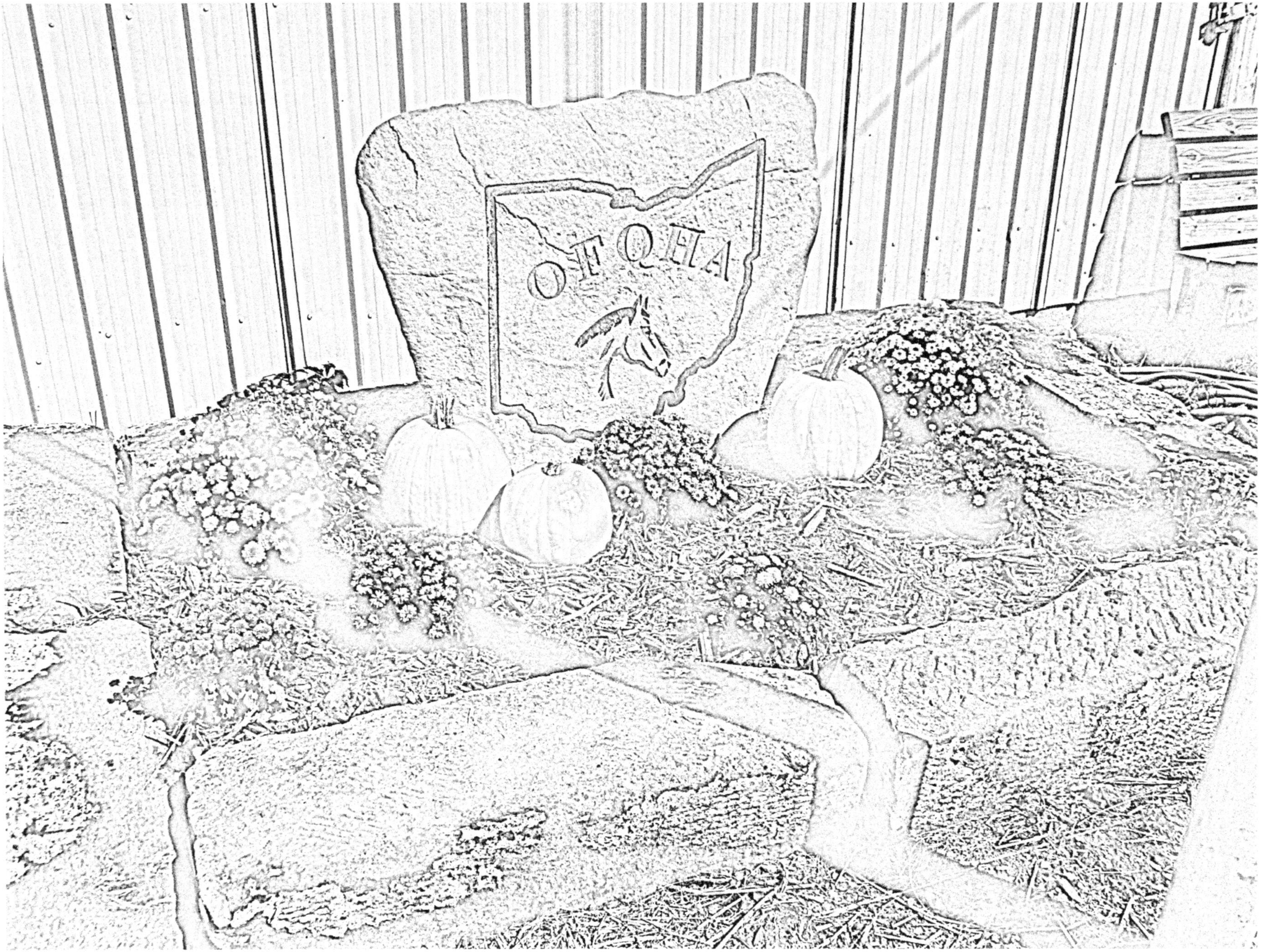
OFQHA

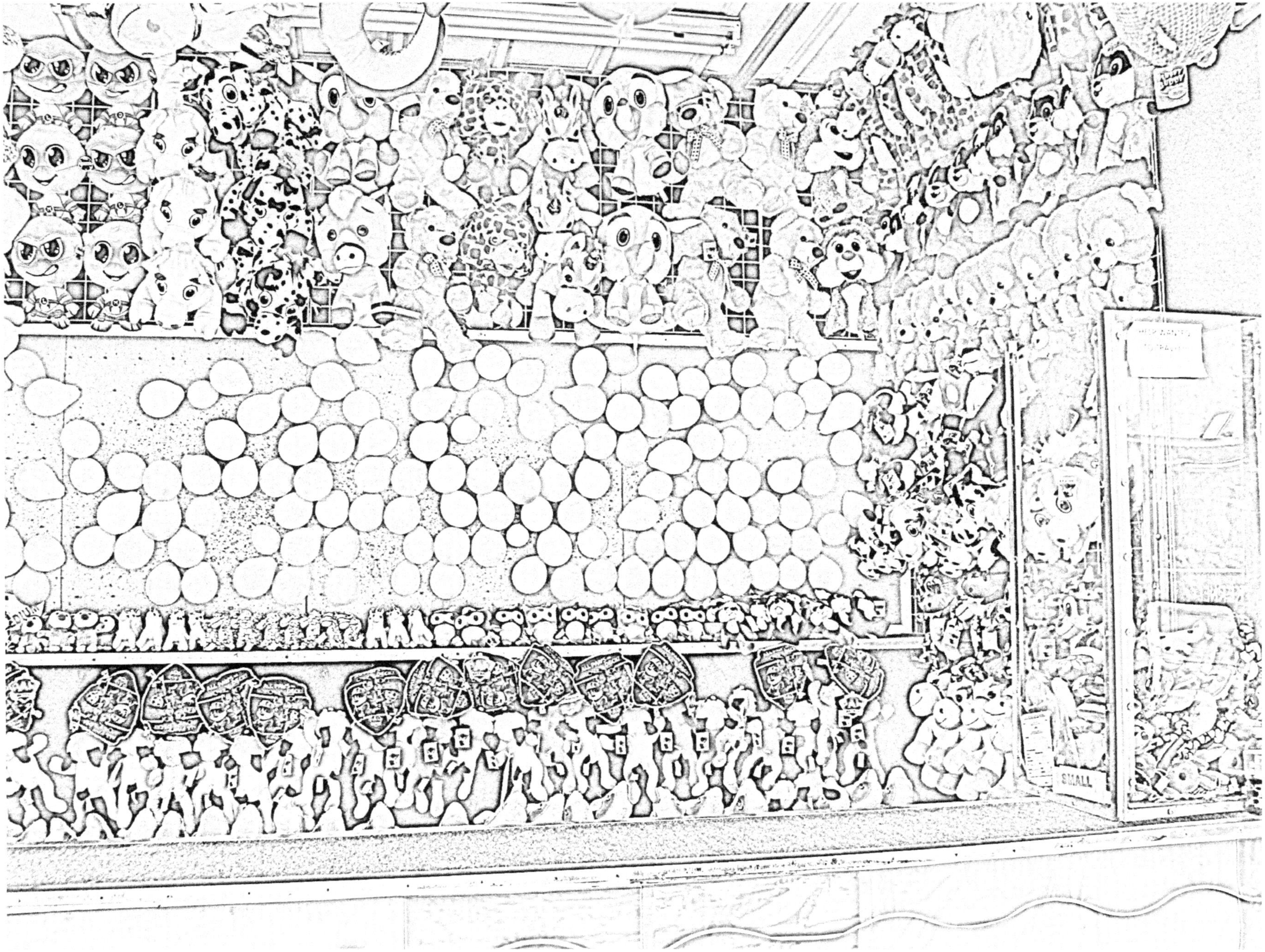
SMALL

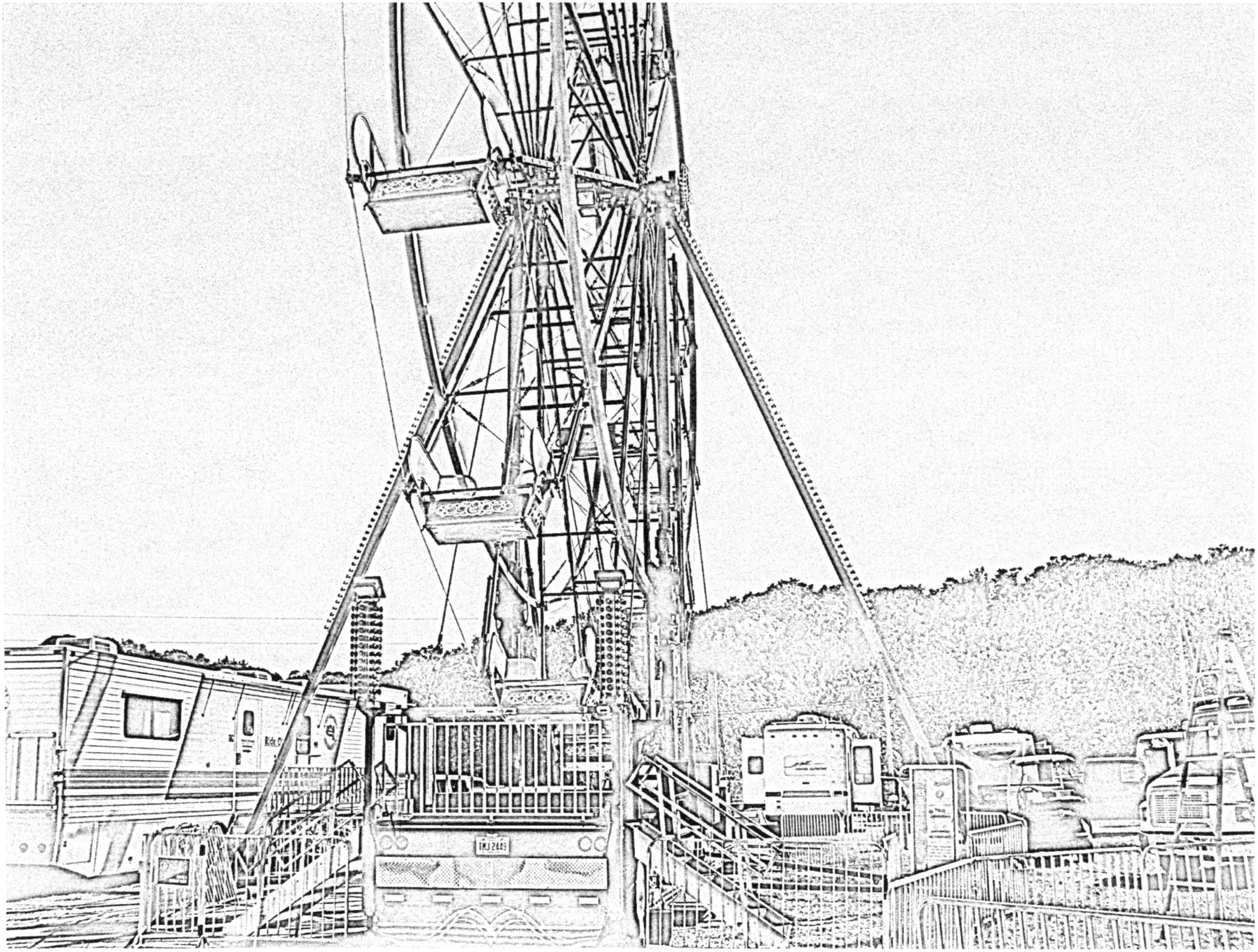

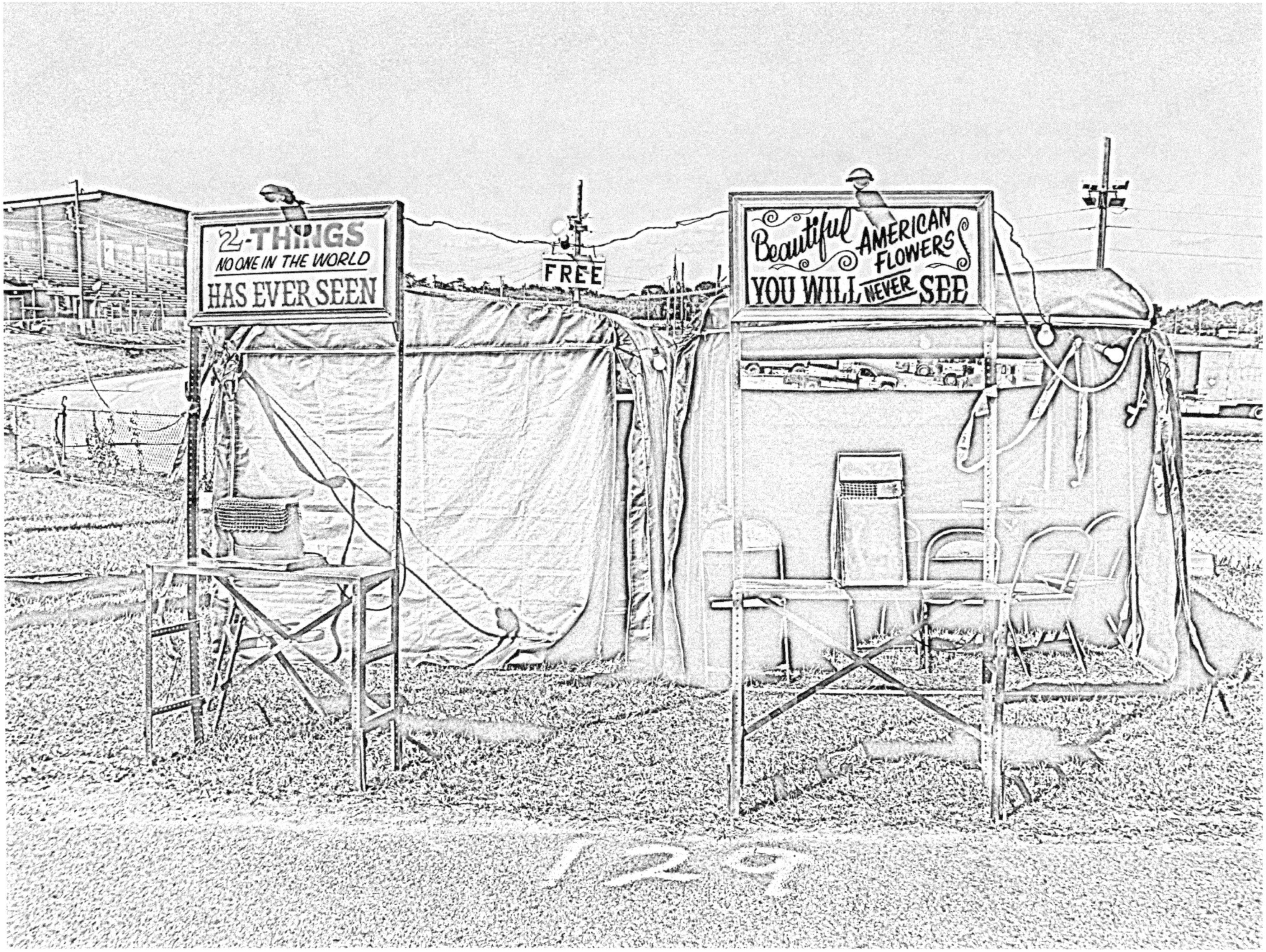
2-THINGS
NO ONE IN THE WORLD
HAS EVER SEEN
FREE
Beautiful AMERICAN FLOWERS
YOU WILL NEVER SEE
129

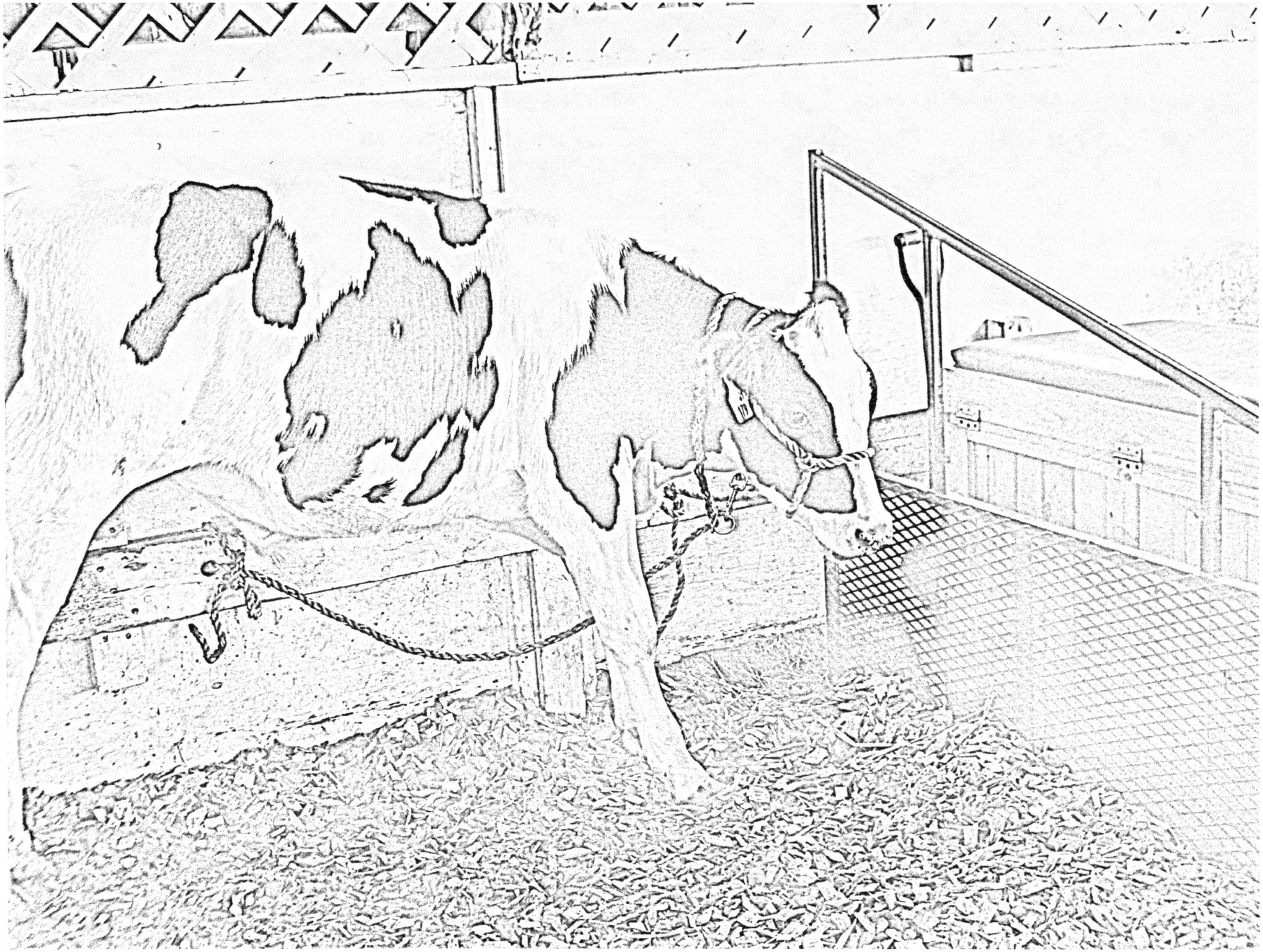

Thank You!
We hope you enjoyed our book.

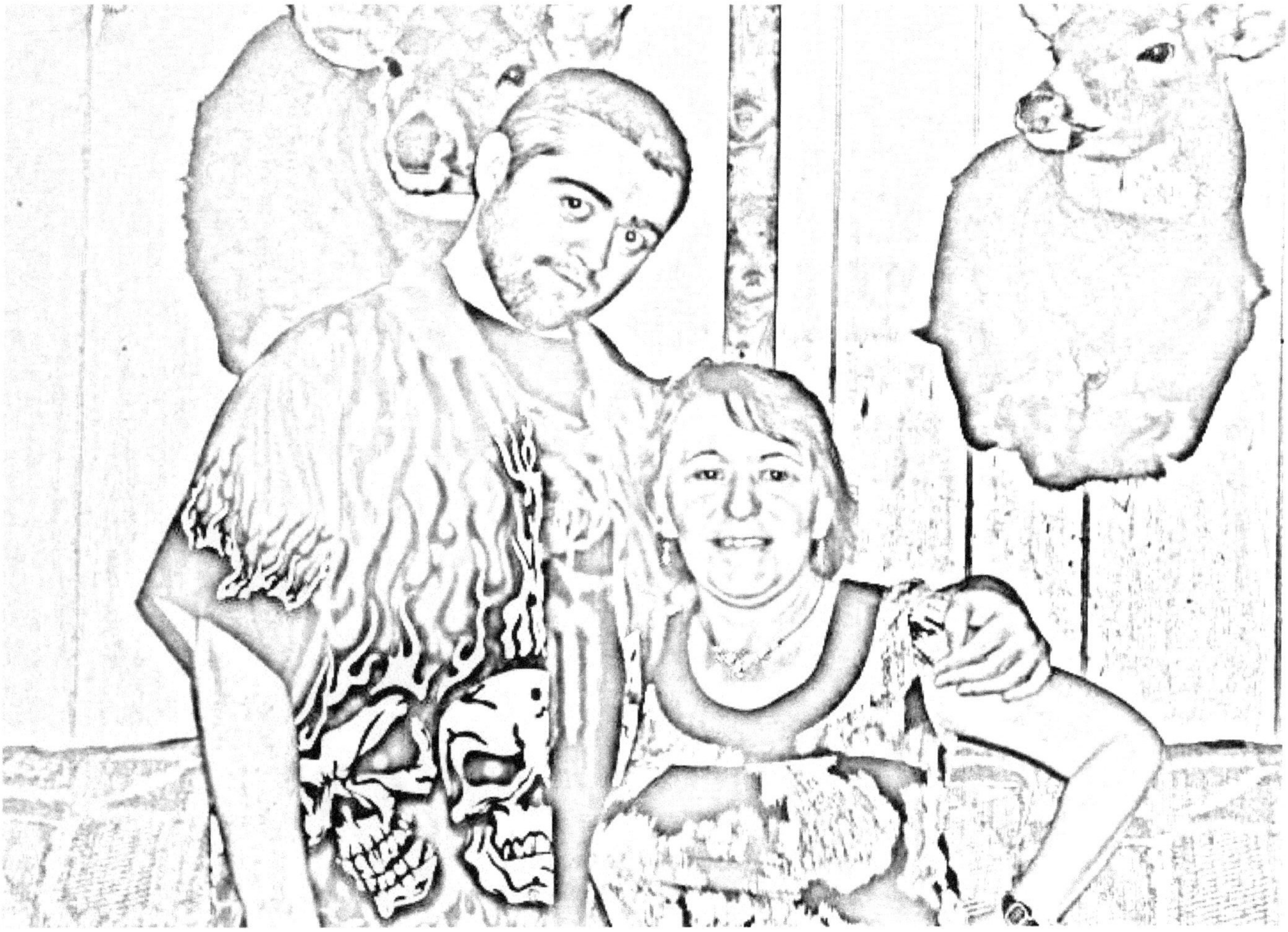

Watch for more coloring books by ARN Arts LLC.
Visit us at: http://arnarts.wixsite.com/books

www.ingramcontent.com/pod-product-compliance
Lightning Source LLC
Chambersburg PA
CBHW080629190526
45169CB00009B/3338
9781539560128